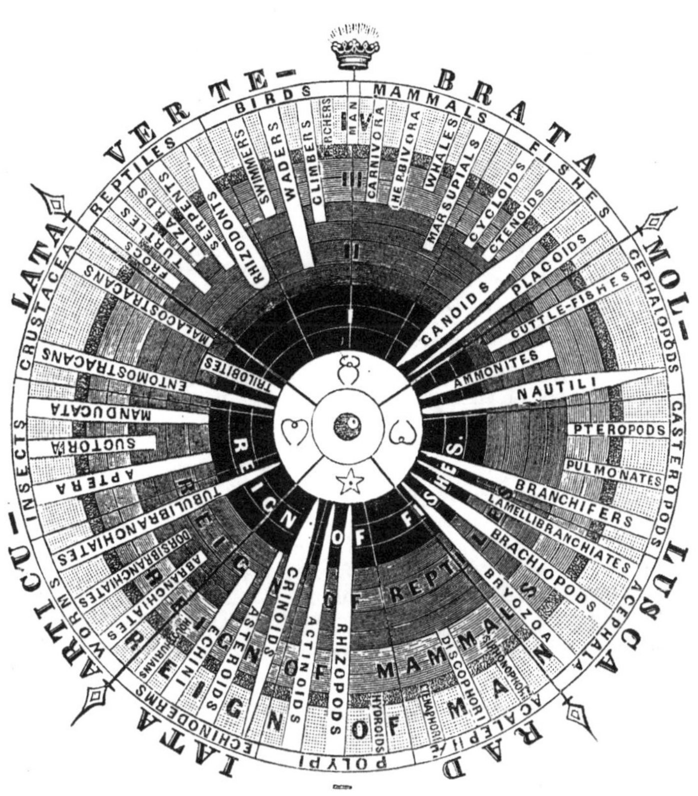

For the use of the above accurate and striking plate, from Agassiz and Gould's Zoology, the author is indebted to those distinguished naturalists.

A WREATH AROUND THE CROSS;

Or Scripture Truths Illustrated. By the REV. A. MORTON BROWN, D. D. With a Recommendatory Preface, by JOHN ANGELL JAMES. With beautiful Frontispiece. 16mo, cloth, 60 cts.

☞ This is a very interesting and valuable book, and should be in every house in the land. Its great excellence is, it *magnifies the cross of Christ.* It presents the following interesting subjects: "The Cross needed; The Way to the Cross; The Cross set up; The sufferings of the Cross Mediation by the Cross; Life from the Cross: Faith in the Cross; Submission to the Cross; Glorying in the Cross; The Cross and the Crown." No better book can be put into the hands of "inquirers after truth.'

This is a beautiful volume, defending and illustrating the precious truths which cluster around the atonement. These truths are set forth in a lively and popular style. — *Phil. Ch. Chronicle.*

May it find its way into every Christian family, and be read by every member. — *Ch. Secretary.*

The theme is the centre of all evangelical religion, both doctrinal and experimental. It is the excellence of this work, that it keeps so constantly in view this grand instrument of salvation, that it might have been entitled a "walk," as well as a "wreath," around the Cross. — *Religious Herald*

"Christ, and Him crucified," is presented in a new, striking: and matter-of-fact light. The style is simple, without being puerile, and the reasoning is of that truthful, persuasive kind that "comes from the heart, and reaches the heart." We wish this Christian classic a wide circulation, hoping that many, under its direction and influence, may be found "looking unto Jesus." — *N. Y. Observer.*

A highly-approved work, issued in elegant style. The author presents the most important doctrines of our holy religion, in a form not only intelligible, but in attractive lights, adapted to allure the eye of faith, and hope, and love to the glorious objects revealed in the gospel. — *Phil. Ch. Observer.*

PHILOSOPHY OF THE PLAN OF SALVATION: A Book for the Times.

By an AMERICAN CITIZEN An Introductory Essay, by CALVIN E. STOWE, D. D. 12mo, cloth, 63 cts.

*** This is one of the best books in the English language. The work has been translated into several different languages in Europe. It has been republished by the London Tract Society, and also adopted as one of the volumes of "Ward's Library of Standard Divinity," edited by Drs. John Harris, J. Pye Smith, and others. A capital book to circulate among young men.

One of the most original and valuable works of recent publication. — *N. Y. Christian Intelligencer.*

A useful book, written with great spirit and point. — *Phil. Presbyterian.*

In many respects, this is a remarkable book. — *N. Y. Observer.*

We have expressed our decided opinion as to the exalted merits of this transatlantic essay on the truth of the Gospel. We think it is more likely to lodge an impression in the human conscience, in favor of the divine authority of Christianity, than any work of the modern press, as it seeks an avenue to the human heart somewhat different from the ordinary mode of approaching it. — *London Meth. Mag.*

It is logical, both in its arrangement and in its reasonings. It is the work of a clear and vigorous thinker It proposes to solve these two questions, — *Is Christianity true?* and, *What is true Christianity?* Few volumes have issued from the American press that bear the stamp of originality and profound thought so deeply imprinted on every page. — *Puritan Rec.*

This is really an original book. Every sentence is pregnant with thought, and every idea conduces to the main demonstration. The various paragraphs are bound together as closely as the successive steps of a mathematical argument. At the same time, neither abstruseness vails the method, nor subtilty polishes away the power of the reasonings employed. Its conclusions come home with certainty to the business and bosom" of every man. The book is the work of a reclaimed sceptic. — *Edinburgh United Secession Magazine.*

Though written with great simplicity, it is evidently the production of a master mind. There is a force of argument and a power of conviction almost resistless. — *London Evangelical Magazine.*

The book before us is one of singular merit. As a piece of clear, vigorous, consecutive thinking, we scarcely know its superior. We would not hesitate to place it side by side with Butler's Analogy, merely as a specimen of close and unanswerable reasoning, while it is far superior with regard to the evangelical view which it gives of the plan of salvation. — *Edinburgh Free Church Magazine.*

"*The president of Knox College, Illinois,*" says, "I have just taken the senior class through the Philosophy of the Plan of Salvation. It is decidedly the best vindication of the Old Testament Scriptures against the assaults of infidelity, and one of the most useful class books which I have ever met."

A Welsh minister, in Michigan, brought a copy from Wales. It has been translated into Welsh, and is circulated broadcast over the hills, through the hamlets, and in the mines of his native land.

IMPORTANT NEW WORKS.

THE CHRISTIAN LIFE: Social and Individual. By PETER BAYNE, A. M. 12mo. Cloth. $1.25.

Contents.—PART I. STATEMENT. I. The Individual Life. II. The Social Life. PART II. EXPOSITION AND ILLUSTRATION. *Book I. Christianity the Basis of Social Life.* I. First Principles. II. Howard; and the rise of Philanthropy. III. Wilberforce; and the development of Philanthropy. IV. Budgett; the Christian Freeman. V. The social problem of the age, and one or two hints towards its solution. *Book II. Christianity the Basis of Individual Character.* I. Introductory: a few Words on Modern Doubt. II. John Foster. III. Thomas Arnold. IV. Thomas Chalmers. PART III. OUTLOOK. I. The Positive Philosophy. II. Pantheistic Spiritualism. III. General Conclusion.

PARTICULAR attention is invited to this work. In Scotland, its publication, during the last winter, produced a great sensation. Hugh Miller made it the subject of an elaborate review in his paper, the Edinburgh *Witness*, and gave his readers to understand that it was an extraordinary work. The "*News of the Churches*," the monthly organ of the Scottish Free Church, was equally emphatic in its praise, pronouncing it "the religious book of the season." Strikingly original in plan and brilliant in execution, it far surpasses the expectations raised by the somewhat familiar title. It is, in truth, a bold onslaught (and the first of the kind) upon the Pantheism of Carlyle, Fichte, etc., by an ardent admirer of Carlyle; and at the same time an exhibition of the Christian Life, in its inner principle, and as illustrated in the lives of Howard, Wilberforce, Budgett, Foster, Chalmers, etc. The brilliancy and vigor of the author's style are remarkable.

PATRIARCHY; or, the Family, its Constitution and Probation. By JOHN HARRIS, D. D., President of "New College," London, and author of "The Great Teacher," "Mammon," "Pre-Adamite Earth," "Man Primeval," etc. 12mo. Cloth. $1.25.

THIS is the third and last of a series, by the same author, entitled "Contributions to Theological Science." The plan of this series is highly original, and thus far has been most successfully executed. Of the first two in the series, "Pre-Adamite Earth," and "Man Primeval," we have already issued four and five editions, and the demand still continues. The immense sale of all Dr. Harris's works attest their intrinsic popularity. The present work has long been expected, but was delayed owing to the author's illness, and the pressure of his duties as President of New College, St. John's Wood. We shall issue it from advanced sheets (a large portion of which have already been received) simultaneously with its publication in England.

GOD REVEALED IN NATURE AND IN CHRIST: Including a Refutation of the Development Theory contained in the "Vestiges of the Natural History of Creation." By the Author of "THE PHILOSOPHY OF THE PLAN OF SALVATION." 12mo. Cloth. $1.25.

THE author of that remarkable book, "The Philosophy of the Plan of Salvation," has devoted several years of incessant labor to the preparation of this work. Without being specifically controversial, its aim is to overthrow several of the popular errors of the day, by establishing the antagonist truth upon an impregnable basis of reason and logic. In opposition to the doctrine of a mere subjective revelation, now so plausibly inculcated by certain eminent writers, it demonstrates the necessity of an external, objective revelation. Especially, it furnishes a new, and as it is conceived, a conclusive argument against the "*development theory*" so ingeniously maintained in the "Vestiges of the Natural History of Creation." As this author does not publish except when he has something to say, there is good reason to anticipate that the work will be one of unusual interest and value. His former book has met with the most signal success in both hemispheres, having passed through numerous editions in England and Scotland, and been translated into four of the European languages besides. It is also about to be translated into the Hindoostanee tongue. (m)

WORKS JUST PUBLISHED.

THE BETTER LAND; or, THE BELIEVER'S JOURNEY AND FUTURE HOME. By REV. A. C. THOMPSON. 12mo, cloth. 85 cents.

CONTENTS. — The Pilgrimage — Clusters of Eschol — Waymarks — Glimpses of the Land — The Passage — The Recognition of Friends — The Heavenly Banquet — Children in Heaven — Society of Angels — Society of the Saviour — Heavenly Honor and Riches — No Tears in Heaven — Holiness of Heaven — Activity in Heaven — Resurrection Body — Perpetuity of Bliss in Heaven.

A most charming and instructive book for all now journeying to the "Better Land."

THE SCHOOL OF CHRIST; or, CHRISTIANITY VIEWED IN ITS LEADING ASPECTS. By the REV. A. L. R. FOOTE, author of "Incidents in the Life of our Saviour," etc. 16mo, cloth.

MEMOIRS OF A GRANDMOTHER. By a Lady of Massachusetts. 16mo, cloth. 50 cents.

"My path lies in a valley which I have sought to adorn with flowers. Shadows from the hills cover it, but I make my own sunshine."

The little volume is gracefully and beautifully written. — *Journal.*

Not unworthy the genius of a Dickens. — *Transcript.*

HOURS WITH EUROPEAN CELEBRITIES. By the REV. WILLIAM B. SPRAGUE, D. D. 12mo, cloth. $1.00. SECOND EDITION.

The author of this work visited Europe in 1828 and in 1836, under circumstances which afforded him an opportunity of making the acquaintance, by personal interviews, of a large number of the most distinguished men and women of that continent; and in his preface he says, "It was my uniform custom, after every such interview, to take copious memoranda of the conversation, including an account of the individual's appearance and manners; in short, defining, as well as I could, the whole impression which his physical, intellectual and moral man had made upon me." From the memoranda thus made, the material for the present instructive and exceedingly interesting volume is derived. Besides these "pen and ink" sketches, the work contains the novel attraction of a fac-simile of the signature of each of the persons introduced.

THE AIMWELL STORIES.

A series of volumes illustrative of youthful character, and combining instruction with amusement. By WALTER AIMWELL, author of "The Boy's Own Guide," "The Boy's Book of Morals and Manners," &c. With numerous Illustrations.

The first three volumes of the series, now ready, are —

OSCAR; or, THE BOY WHO HAD HIS OWN WAY. 16mo, cloth, gilt. 63 cents.

CLINTON; or, BOY-LIFE IN THE COUNTRY. 16mo, cloth, gilt. 63 cents.

ELLA; or, TURNING OVER A NEW LEAF. 16mo, cloth, gilt. 63 cents.

☞ Each volume will be complete and independent of itself, but the series will be connected by a partial identity of character, localities, &c.

THE PLURALITY OF WORLDS. A NEW EDITION. With a SUPPLEMENTARY DIALOGUE, in which the author's reviewers are reviewed. 12mo, cloth. $1

This masterly production, which has excited so much interest in this country and in Europe, will now have an increased attraction in the addition of the Supplement, in which the author's reviewers are triumphantly reviewed.

☞ The Supplement will be furnished separate to those who have the original work.

INFLUENCE OF THE HISTORY OF SCIENCE UPON INTELLECTUAL EDUCATION. By WILLIAM WHEWELL, D. D., of Trinity College, Cambridge, Eng., and the alleged author of "Plurality of Worlds." 16mo, cloth. 25 cts

THE LANDING AT CAPE ANNE; or, THE CHARTER OF THE FIRST PERMANENT COLONY ON THE TERRITORY OF THE MASSACHUSETTS COMPANY. Now discovered and first published from the ORIGINAL MANUSCRIPT, with an inquiry into its authority, and a HISTORY OF THE COLONY, 1624-1628. Roger Conant Governor. By JOHN WINGATE THORNTON. 8vo, cloth. $1.50.

This is a curious and exceedingly valuable historical document.

A volume of great interest and importance. — *Evening Traveller.*

GOD REVEALED IN NATURE AND IN CHRIST.—In the title page of this volume (published by GOULD & LINCOLN) the author of the "Philosophy of the Plan of Salvation" announces himself to the public. The Rev. James B. Walker, of Mansfield, Ohio, a Congregational pastor, claims the honor of that work as well as of this.

The work now before us is a contribution at once to natural theology and to the evidences of the Christian revelation. It attempts to trace out not only the evidences of creation and of an intelligent Creator, but also the indications of the character of God that are given in the known laws, tendencies and progress of the world. It deals with facts much more recondite than those which are the basis of the argument in the same author's former work; and therefore it requires in the reader a closer attention, and a higher degree of general knowledge, than are necessary in studying the other. Chemistry and geology, especially the latter, are employed effectively in the argument against the most recent forms of atheism. Profound analogies between the laws of the material universe, and the laws of God's moral government are strikingly illustrated.

It was not until the "Philosophy of the Plan of Salvation" had acquired reputation in England, that it begun to be appreciated in this country. Meanwhile, the author had parted with his interest in the copyright for a trifling consideration. Perhaps we may render a service to the American public by informing them that this new work is already published on the other side of the water in two editions, and that the sale of this American work on natural theology, is there a hundred times greater than the sale of the Aberdeen Burnet prize essays on the same subject.

SACRED PHILOSOPHY.

GOD REVEALED

IN THE

PROCESS OF CREATION,

AND BY THE

MANIFESTATION OF JESUS CHRIST;

INCLUDING AN

EXAMINATION OF THE DEVELOPMENT THEORY

CONTAINED IN THE

"VESTIGES OF THE NATURAL HISTORY OF CREATION."

BY

JAMES B. WALKER,

AUTHOR OF "PHILOSOPHY OF THE PLAN OF SALVATION."

BOSTON:

GOULD AND LINCOLN,

59 WASHINGTON STREET.

NEW YORK: SHELDON, LAMPORT & BLAKEMAN,

115 NASSAU STREET.

1855.

CONTENTS.

BOOK ONE.

CHAPTER I.

CHAPTER II.

CHAPTER III.

CHAPTER IV.

CHAPTER V

CHAPTER VI.

CHAPTER VII.

CHAPTER VIII.

CHAPTER IX.

BOOK TWO.

OF MAN AND HIS RESPONSIBILITIES, CONSIDERED IN CONNECTION WITH DIVINE LAW AND DIVINE REVELATION.

CHAPTER I.

CHAPTER II.

CHAPTER III.

CHAPTER IV.

CHAPTER V.

CHAPTER VI.

CHAPTER VII.

ADDENDUM.

INTRODUCTION.

ALL the Bridgewater Treatises aim to develop the central idea in Natural Theology—that design, apparent in the phenomena of creation, indicates an intelligent Designer. In the work of Chalmers some new strength has been added to the argument for the *moral character* of the Supreme Architect. These treatises are able and discriminating, each marching through a different province of science to the same grand conclusion. By a few these volumes will always be appreciated; but we fear little has been added by their publication to the popular religious conviction of Christendom beyond what had been produced by the work of Paley. And, indeed, it is doubtful whether any work, predicated solely upon the deductions of Natural Theology, can add much to the strength of the persuasion, possessed in common by all men, that a Supreme Being exists and reigns over the universe.

What the world needs, is not so much evidence of the *existence* of a Supreme Being, as evidence of the *moral character* of the Creator—evidence of the *moral aim* and *end* of the *Divine Plan*—evidence not only "that God *is*," but also "that he is a REWARDER *of those who diligently seek him.*" This has been the actual point of conflict between the unbelievers and the faithful in all the ages of revelation.

Soon after the Bridgewater Treatises were published, the book known as the "Philosophy of the Plan of Salvation" made its appearance in America, and was immediately republished in England. It intimated in its preface the opinion of its author, that the Bridgewater books did not meet the want of the times. They did not answer to the great question which the inquiring reason of the civilized world propounds. Men might read them all, and go forth more skeptical in relation to revealed religion than before. The very fact that the vital question had not been discussed might indicate to the philosophic skeptic that it could not be maintained upon the basis of a sound philosophy, nor by the processes of rational induction.

Deeply sensible, therefore, that the Bridgewater Treatises, whatever they might be in other respects, had failed upon the main issue, the author of the "Philosophy of the Plan of Salvation" aimed to do what they had not done—to identify the God of the Creation with the God of the Bible, and the first principles of Christianity with the canons of human reason. He aimed to show, by the same process by which the conclusions of Natural Theology are reached, that the Mosaic and Christian Dispensations are the work of the same Mind that planned and developed the Physical Creation. This is the question of the Christian Ages

—this the demand made upon the Christian theists of our own time.

That the Author did not misconceive the want of the times, nor fail in some measure to meet it, is evident from the fact, that his book is sold by thousands of volumes, while technical works on Natural Theology (Paley always excepted) live only in professional libraries. It is studied in many of the seminaries of Great Britain and America—has been translated into all the principal languages of the Continent—is about to be translated into Hindoostanee, and at the present time is extending its influence more widely than ever before.

The success of his first volume has stimulated the Author to give to the public another volume—a second "Book for the Times"—at a period when he thinks the state of the question in Europe and America calls for its circulation.

Recently, a series of essays have been written for the prize offered at Aberdeen, which includes both Nature and Revelation in the same thesis. It is hoped that they may be books which will live; but previous experience in connection with the same prize awakens the fear that they may be able and formal discussions, like their predecessors, which will fail to awaken an interest in the public mind, or to attract the attention of inquirers for truth; and hence fail to promote by an extended influence the honor of Christ and the spiritual good of men.

We have here, therefore, a second treatise from the Author of the "Philosophy of the Plan of Salvation;" not an introduction to the first book, nor a sequel, but a Companion; in which the argument of the previous work is extended and strengthened. The Supreme Being, as revealed in Nature and Revelation, is exhibited, not only as the Author of the physical and moral systems of the universe; but a chief and further aim of the volume is to exhibit the Unity of the Divine Plan, physical and moral, upon our planet, and the process through which it has passed, and by which it is progressing to ultimate perfection. In this volume the unity of the physical and spiritual scheme of the Creator, as it has been developed in our world, we think is established; and the *final end* of the whole plan of the mundane economy is shown to be moral in its nature, and the same as those revealed in the Christian Scriptures.

To the skeptic, the candid inquirer, and the Christian, we commend the book, hoping that, like its predecessor, it may interest and benefit many readers.

⁂ A condensed statement of facts and principles is given in the first chapters of the work. This is done in order to the completeness of the book in itself—to give the general reader an apprehension of what is admitted to be the present state of the discussion, and to furnish an intelligent introduction to the argument which follows.

BOOK ONE.

"I ENVY NO QUALITY OF MIND OR INTELLECT IN OTHERS, BE IT GENIUS, POWER, WIT, OR FANCY; BUT IF I COULD CHOOSE WHAT WOULD BE MOST DELIGHTFUL, AND, I BELIEVE, MOST USEFUL TO ME, I SHOULD PREFER A FIRM RELIGIOUS BELIEF TO EVERY OTHER BLESSING: FOR IT MAKES LIFE A DISCIPLINE OF GOODNESS—CREATES NEW HOPES WHEN ALL EARTHLY HOPES VANISH—THROWS OVER THE DECAY, THE DESTRUCTION OF EXISTENCE, THE MOST GORGEOUS OF ALL LIGHTS—AWAKENS LIFE IN DEATH—AND FROM CORRUPTION AND DECAY CALLS UP BEAUTY AND DIVINITY."

SIR HUMPHRY DAVY.

CHAPTER I.

PRELIMINARY STATEMENT OF FIRST TRUTHS.

In an argument deduced from the Light of Nature for the Being of God, nothing can be properly assumed in the outset except those first truths which are revealed in the human consciousness. The existence of Mind is implied in the act of thinking, and there are certain laws of mind which are implied in the process of reasoning; and however men may differ about *first knowledge*, or *certain knowledge* of things external to the mind itself, yet all agree that we must doubt the veracity—or rather, that we must affirm the fallacy—of sensation, before we can doubt the existence of phenomena external to the mind.

I am:—The external world is:—In all sane minds these elementary convictions exist; and they are assumed in all processes of the reason. It is not possible for a man to act as though he doubted either the existence of self or of the external world. Men may adopt hypotheses which will lead them to propound doubts upon this subject, but no man can act upon the supposition that such doubts are valid. We can not think without being conscious of our existence; we can not act without being conscious of motion and matter external to the self of the mind. The *subjective* and the *objective*—the *me* and the *not me*—are correlated and co-existing intuitions, revealed in the consciousness of all intelligent active beings.

The mind is not only conscious of the existence of self, and the existence of the external world, but every mind affirms of itself that the external world—its forms and movements—*are not dependent upon me.* By this inter-action of the subjective and the objective the idea or notion of *Cause and Effect* is produced. By cause and effect, as thus perceived, we do not merely understand the succession of antecedent and sequence; but properly, cause and effect: the effect being connected as a *con*sequence with its cause.

That the idea of cause and effect is connate with the exercise of the reason, is manifest from several considerations. It is seen in the fact that men have universally, and in all ages, assumed that forms and changes in nature have a cause. Those who have assumed that matter is eternal, have yet assumed causation as precedent to the modifications of matter. Skepticism in relation to this elementary law of the reason is scarcely possible. Insanity often consists in assuming inadequate or absurd causes; but this, of itself, shows that a first and necessary element of the reason consists in assuming adequate and rational causes for all perceived phenomena. Thus, whether in a normal or an abnormal condition, there exists in the human mind the elementary conviction of cause and effect; and the normal or sane condition of mind is indicated by the assumption of adequate and rational causes for the various forms and changes which the creation exhibits to the senses.

By endeavoring to form the idea of an effect, or change of form, without a cause, every one may be conscious of the intuitive character of the conviction of causation. We may vary the notion of an effect, and vary its name, but we can form no idea of an effect existing without an efficient antecedent of some sort. The conviction, then, that every effect is related to an adequate cause, is an element of mind so far that without it there can be no sane intellect. The correlation of cause and effect is a primary truth, the assumption of which lies at the basis of all processes of the reason.

THE INQUIRY OF THE DISCUSSION STATED.

These first truths introduce us into the field of inquiry, the exploration of which is proposed in the first part of the following discussion. The process of the discussion may be such as to allow the most ample statement. Is the external world, as known to us, uncaused or self-caused? or is it the effect of a separate cause, adequate to the production of the perceived phenomena? All the phases of the main inquiry are included in this—Is there a FIRST CAUSE, adequate in power, intelligence, and goodness, to whom we must attribute the production of the phenomena of the universe, so far as known to us?

The idea of God, as revealed by the Light of Nature, can not be less than that of a cause adequate to the production of all the phenomena known to us. The true idea of God may signify more than this, because our knowledge of the universe is limited in extent, and in many cases our apprehensions of natural phenomena are inaccurate. The more discriminating, therefore, the examination of the parts, relations, and processes of created things, and the more comprehensive the induction of natural phenomena, the greater will be the probability of approximating, by correct reasonings, to a knowledge of the existence and character of God.

The testimonies, likewise, for the existence and government of the Supreme Being, will be strengthened in proportion as we are able to derive the same conclusion from many different premises. The eduction of a general result from many conclusions logically accumulated is, perhaps, the highest and most satisfactory evidence that can be presented to the mind of man, in relation to the subject under consideration.

"Organization implies law." This truth is conceded as the basis of all science. Whether it be argued that the law is coeval with the organization, or produces or governs the organization by a force of nature, or by the will of God—whatever view is taken of the causal energy, still it is conceded as a tenet of human knowledge that organization implies law, by which the form and changes of the organism are governed.

THE POINT OF BEGINNING.

Recent studies of the physical history of the earth have established the fact, that in the process of creation, either by the development or introduction of species, vegetable and animal life have advanced upon the scale of creation, from lower to higher forms. This fact points us to the first ascertained step in creative progress as the point where we should begin our inquiries. We shall gain some advantage by directing our train of thought in accordance with the "course of creation," as it rises from first to last things. If the footsteps of the Creator, proceeding from the vast obscure, become more visible when life dawns in organic forms upon the earth, then, by following those footprints, we shall certainly travel in the direction in which Creative Energy and Wisdom have proceeded; and we trust we shall gather by the way satisfactory evidence of the existence and character of the Creating Mind.

We assume, then, subjectively, the existence of mind, and of the primary laws which govern the reason;—objectively, the existence of matter, and of law governing the changes of material phenomena. And we commence our inquiries with the facts which form the earliest reliable knowledge of the earth's history.

CHAPTER II.

INTRODUCTORY.

THE PRESENT POSITION AND BEARINGS OF THE ARGUMENT STATED.

THE Ancients, who assumed that creation from nothing was an impossibility, did not infer therefrom that there were no gods. Many profound thinkers assumed that both Matter and Spirit had existed from eternity. Whether, with Aristotle, they supposed the union of spirit and matter a necessity of things; or whether they believed, as the Epicureans taught, that there was a Divine Mind separate from matter; or with Plato, that the union of spirit with matter was a voluntary influx of the Infinite One, pervading the forms and producing the motions of matter; still, in one view or another, the prevailing sentiments of the ancients was, that both Mind and Matter were uncreated entities.

The Moderns have held a different opinion. With the exception of the school of Spinosa, and slight modifications of his views by men of more recent times, philosophers generally have adopted, and endeavored to sustain, the opinion that matter is a created substance. It is believed that this doctrine is taught in the Sacred Scriptures; and hence an impression has prevailed, that skeptical opinions are encouraged by hypotheses all which do not accord with that interpretation of Genesis which teaches the creation of matter out of nothing by the omnific word of God.

In our own times, the assumption that matter is a created substance is not held to be either so sacred or so important as it was formerly supposed to be. Some modern authors have endeavored to show that the creation spoken of in Genesis refers only to the existing order of things—the formation of matter into the various species of organized life. Others find, in the first verse of Genesis, an announcement of the creation of matter ages anterior to the formation of the organic kingdoms of nature. This last opinion is at present, probably, the prevailing one, sustained by more influential names* and by a better scriptural exegesis than any other.

THE QUESTION WHETHER MATTER BE A CREATED SUBSTANCE—NOT ESSENTIAL.

On the subject of the creation of matter, Dr. Chalmers is a good exponent of the views of those writers

* Buckland, Chalmers, Pye Smith, Hitchcock.

who seek data both in natural and revealed theology. This able theologian, while he maintains that there are good reasons to support the opinion that matter is a created substance, yet denies that the question is one of importance in the study of natural theology:—"The palpable argument for the being of God, as grounded on the phenomena of visible nature, lies not in the existence of matter, but in the arrangements of its parts—a firmer stepping-stone to the conclusion than the mere entity of that which is corporeal to the previous entity of that which is spiritual. To us it marks far more intelligently the voice of a God, to have called forth the beauteous and beneficent order of our world from the womb of chaos, than to have called forth the substance of our world from the chambers of nonentity. We know that the voice of God called forth both, but it is one of those voices which sounds so audibly and distinctly in reason's ear. Of the other we have been told, and we think needed to have been told, by Revelations."* He adds—"The question to be resolved then is, not whether the *matter of the world*, but whether the *present order of the world* had a commencement."

An American writer, eminent in his own country,

* Natural Theology, b. i. c. 5.

and not unknown in Europe,* says—"We must confess at the outset, that Geology furnishes no more evidence than the other sciences of the creation of the matter of the universe out of nothing; but it does furnish us with examples of such modifications of matter as could be effected only by a Deity." Thus good writers concur, that in the scientific argument for the being of God, the question concerning the eternity of matter may be set aside, as not essential to the strength or validity of their conclusions.

Yet, if this question be held in abeyance, it is not thereby conceded that matter is an uncreated substance. A position of uncertain value is not contested; but it is never supposed that the waving of the discussion on this subject weakens the strength or affects the foundation of the evidence that there is a God who created and who governs the world. It is only supposed that it removes the basis of the argument from a more obscure to a more clear and firm position—from the region of assumption and *à priori* argumentation to the premises of rational and *à posteriori* induction.

OPINIONS AND DISCRIMINATIONS CONCERNING THE LAWS OF MATTER.

The question concerning the laws of matter is more complicated and difficult than that concerning the

* Hitchcock's Religion and Geology, p. 162.

creation of matter. This question in some form has entered as an element into the inquiries of all ages concerning the being of God. Some views of the nature of law, and of the place which the term claims in the argument, are defined; but much obscurity rests on this topic because of erroneous or imperfect definitions. It will be our aim in the progress of this treatise to elucidate this subject. Meanwhile, there are some things in the present state of opinions which it will aid us to notice, as introductory to future inquiries.

In many writers of the skeptical school, such phrases as the "laws of matter" and the "nature of things" have a significance of the highest import. In the estimation of such authors as Le Compte and Mirabaud, these phrases designate natural causes adequate to the production of all the visible phenomena of nature. Materialists of this class are understood to deny the existence of a personal God. This opinion some expressly avow. Others, however, who profess to find in nature an adequate cause for all the forms and changes which matter assumes, yet introduce phraseology which recognizes a personal creating mind;* and it is prob-

* The whole revelation of the works of God presented to our senses is a system based, *from* what we are compelled, for want of a better term, to call *law;* by which, however, is *not meant a system* independent of or ex-

ably but right to suppose that this phraseology gives their true convictions, notwithstanding their theories and their logic seem to maintain a different conclusion. But, although the naturalistic writers differ among themselves in regard to the existence of a personal God, yet all of them agree in finding a sufficient cause for existing phenomena in some pre-existing condition of nature, without the intervention of any power superior to matter and its laws.

The indefinite apprehension and use of such phrases as those referred to, has greatly retarded the progress of true philosophy.* That the laws of matter are as old as matter itself—that organic laws are as old as organization, no one doubts. But when organic laws are spoken of as causing organization, and the nature of things as giving a nature to things, effects are confounded with causes, and the whole course of the reasoning is vitiated.

Professor Whewell has made some valuable discriminations between the laws of matter and the collocations of matter—between the laws and the "rules" or "adaptations" observed in the relations and *modus operandi* of these laws. By the labors of the Bridge-

clusive of the Deity, but one which only proposes a certain mode of his working.—*Sequel to Vestiges of Creation.*

* Sir J. Herschel's Address, 1845.

water writers, the argument has been cleared of many extraneous and unnecessary *excurses*. Admitting that law governs not only the movements, but that it is coeval with the constitution of things, the evidences of a designing mind are found in the manner in which matter is located in time and space, and in the adaptation by which things are formed in combination with the laws of matter and the laws of life. The existence of God is not argued so much from the mere existence, either of matter or law, as from the apparent design in adjusting the laws and forms of matter, in such ways as that, by the interworking of the collocated economy, specific and valuable ends are produced.

"The watchmaker did not give its elasticity to the mainspring, nor its regularity to the balance-wheel, nor its transparency to the glass, nor the momentum of its varying forces to the mechanism; yet the whole is replete with marks of intelligence, announcing throughout the adjusting and forming skill of a maker, who had an eye on all these properties, and assigned the right place and adjustment to each of them, in fashioning and bringing together the parts of an instrument for the measurement and indication of time. Now the same distinction can be observed in all the specimens of natural mechanism. It is true that we credit the author with the creation and laws of matter as well as its dispositions; but this does not hinder its being in the latter, and not in the former, where the manifestations of skill are most apparent, or where the chief argument for a Divinity lies."*

The foregoing extract is a good condensation of the opinions of modern writers on this point. The agency and wisdom of the Infinite Architect are seen, not so much in the law of refraction, or in the reflective surface of a lens, or in the contractile structure of a muscle, nor in the motive power of osseous lever, nor in the form of one or all of these; but when the lenses and laws are adjusted in definite relations—when the contractile muscle moves the machinery in adaptation to external objects disconnected from the machine itself, and all these parts, and processes, and laws are balanced and worked together as one particular mechanism, correlated to many others in and out of the human system—from this collocation of parts, and adjustment of laws to parts, are deduced the agency, and wisdom, and goodness of the Divine Mind.

Thus, while Theists hold that the existence of God may be inferred from the existence of matter and the

* Chalmer's Nat. The. b. ii. c. 1.

laws of matter, yet they take their main position where the reason grasps the material with clearer apprehension, and where the argument rests upon the basis of a broader induction.

CHAPTER III.

SUMMARY OF THE ARGUMENT FROM FIRST THINGS.

ALTHOUGH the question concerning the eternity of matter is held in abeyance by able theologians, and the argument deducible from the existence of the laws of matter is not so much insisted upon by others, yet, there is a testimony deducible from the existence and properties of first things which indicates the personal existence of God.

To the minds of many, whose competency to judge in the case no one will doubt, there is much weight in the testimony for the wisdom and goodness of God, which is derived from the ultimate proportion and properties of matter.

The researches of such experimenters as Lussac and Thompson have revealed facts formerly unknown concerning the primary elements and properties of things. In order to give the general reader the basis of the argument now under review, we will exhibit a brief exposition of principles which will be assented to by most or all scientific inquirers.

FORMS AND FORCES OF ELEMENTARY ATOMS.

About sixty elementary bodies have been discovered. Each of these is composed of atoms identical in nature —almost infinitely small, and yet of definite size and gravity. These elementary atoms are governed by certain laws which regulate their motive forces, the most prominent of which are chemical affinity, cohesion, and polarization. At certain degrees of temperature, most, if not all the elementary substances, will combine with others, and form compounds. We rarely find in nature any of the elementary principles in a separate state. Alone they seem to be restless, and to seek by an innate affinity, or *virtus*, equilibrium, or rest, in union with atoms of other elementary substances. The strength of affinity which holds the elementary atoms of different substances in union with each other, is stronger in some cases than others. The attraction between oxygen and potassium is so strong that if a portion of potassium be thrown into a portion of water combustion is produced : the oxygen of the water separates from the hydrogen, unites with the potassium, and leaves the hydrogen free.

The union of elementary substances takes place according to a law of definite proportions—proportions definite both in volume and weight.

The bodies which are formed by the union of elementary atoms with each other are called binary or primary compounds. One binary compound often unites with others; thus forming complex or ternary compounds; as when an acid which is composed of two elementary substances unites with an alkaline base, which is a binary compound of another character.

In the formation of these chemical compounds the elementary molecules, as we have noticed, unite with each other in definite proportions. If the chemist experiments with 1000 parts, by weight, of the chloride of sodium (common salt), he will obtain 600 parts of chlorine, a greenish vapor, and 400 parts of sodium, a white shining solid. This would be the invariable product of the analysis.

In common chalk—the carbonate of lime (or more accurately, the carbonate of the oxyd of lime)—the chemist has a ternary or complex compound. Two binary compounds, carbonic acid and the oxyd of calcium, unite in its formation. 1000 parts of chalk will yield in the first analysis 440 parts of carbonic acid and 560 parts of lime. The complex compound is now separated into two primary compounds—carbonic acid and lime. The chemist pursues the analysis, and obtains the elementary substances in each of these, in the proportion of 320 parts of oxygen and 120 parts of carbon, in the carbonic acid—a proportion of 3 to 8. From the lime he obtains 160 parts of oxygen and 400 parts of calcium—a proportion of 2 to 5.

If, now, the experimenter, having obtained the elementary substances, desires to compound them again, he can do it only in definite weights. Thus analytic and synthetic processes demonstrate the principle of definite proportion in the primary atoms of matter.

As in gravity, so in volume; the elementary substances unite in definite proportions. To form water, half the bulk and eight times the weight of oxygen unite with twice the bulk and eight times the weight of hydrogen.

One substance will often take two or more proportions of some other into union with itself, one quantity being a serial or multiple proportion of the other. The gases, oxygen and nitrogen, unite in the following several proportions: 14 of oxygen to 8 of hydrogen; 14—24; 14—32; 14—40. Fourteen parts of nitrogen will receive from one to five times the definite proportion of eight of oxygen.

These elementary atoms of about sixty different substances, united in different proportions, form the visible phenomena of the globe. By homogeneous attraction elementary masses are formed—by elective attraction compound bodies are formed; the latter affinity regulated by the principle of proportion, as exhibited by the foregoing facts.

Sir John Herschel, before the Royal Society in 1845, in noticing these facts, said—"These discoveries effectually destroy the idea of an external self-existent matter, by giving to each of its atoms at once the essential characteristics of a manufactured article and a subordinate agent." "When we see," says he, "a great number of things precisely alike, we do not believe this similarity to have originated except from a common principle independent of them." These remarks indicate the character of the argument, and the conclusion fairly deducible from the nature and properties of first things.

ADDITIONAL INFERENCES DEDUCIBLE FROM THE SAME FACTS.

There are other considerations in addition to those spoken of by Sir John, which render the argument derived from the forms and properties of primitive atoms almost as satisfactory, to some minds, as that predicated upon evidences of design in the structure of animated beings; and, being the last step in the ascending scale from effect to cause, the argument is the more conclusive. If there be marks of design in the form and qualities of first things, there is no intervening second cause between them and the Creator. From this last step in the *à posteriori* argument we ascend directly to the Creating Mind. With the primary properties of matter second causes cease, and the forms and forces of first things stand connected, by a logical necessity, immediately with the First Cause.

We will notice other marks of design besides those referred to above, which may be gathered from the primitive constitution of things.

Instead of a single elementary principle, about sixty, more or less, are known to exist.* These being diverse in their nature from each other—*one not being produced from the other*, and *yet all bearing the evidence of relation to one another*—this diversity of properties and unity of relations brings in each additional element, after the first, as an additional evidence of the existence of a Designing Creator. Had there been but one, or even two or three elementary substances, the organized kingdoms of nature could not have existed. Every additional element therefore which aids to constitute the variety, and which is necessary to constitute the forms of life, is an evidence of a Designing Intelli-

* The question concerning further divisibility of some substances now supposed to be elementary does not affect the argument. Should the supposition prove true, it would increase rather than diminish its force. It would increase the plurality in the premises, and thereby strengthen the calculation against the doctrine of chance.

gence, exercised in view of the future organic orders of nature, ages before they were called into existence.

The fluidity of some elementary substances, and the solid and gaseous character of others, in their natural state, show another adaptation in the form of first things. If the elements were all solids or all fluids, no organized being could exist. We know it is sometimes said, in answer to such statements as this, that organized beings might exist in such conditions, only they would be differently constituted from present species, and adapted to the condition of universal fluidity or solidity. But there are necessities even in the nature of things. There could have been no body without solidity, and no motion of bodies without fluid or gaseous elements. The supposition, therefore, is absurd; and the evidence of design seen in the solid, fluid, and gaseous constitution of elementary substances, stands unimpeached.

These testimonies are cumulative. When we add to this diversity in the natural state of the elements their capacity to change from solids to fluids, and *vice versâ*, the evidence of design, seen in the relation of one of these characteristics to the other, and of all to the varied phenomena of nature, is strengthened many fold.

Again: There are, as we have noticed, two species of attraction; the one uniting homogeneous atoms—

the other forming compounds of diverse substances into one mass. Now, had but one attractive force characterized matter, the earth would have continued forever without form, and void. With but one attractive force, homogeneous masses would have been formed: but these masses would have existed in an isolated state; and in this condition, if there were movement of the elementary masses, it would have occasioned the eternal collision and repellence of isolated substances. But by an additional attraction, which unites the essential elements of matter with each other, in bodies whose compounds are almost infinitely varied, place, and form, and beauty are given to the animate and inanimate phenomena of the creation.

Again: The proportionate volume and gravity of elementary molecules furnishes another evidence of design in the beginning of the creation. Suppose there had been no fixed proportion regulating the union of oxygen and nitrogen, but that they would mix with each other in any and in all proportions; then there could have been no adjustment of the lungs of animated beings to the atmosphere. Proportion in the one was necessary, in order that there could be adaptation and adjustment in the other. So of other compounds which affect other parts and processes of the animal economy. If there had been no definite proportions, in which alone the elementary substances would compound themselves, there could have been no adjustment of the organs of motion and life to the conditions of nature.

THESE SEVERAL CONSIDERATIONS ACCUMULATE A STRONG TESTIMONY.

Now, when all these particulars are contemplated in their relations to each other, the conclusion seems almost irresistible, that the physical creation at its birth was endowed with proportions, and properties, and laws, which implied, as a sequence, the organic creation, yet many ages in the future. A creation of first things with such a constitution contains evidence in itself (as we think) of the creation of matter, and most certainly of the power and wisdom of God in giving form, property, and law to the material universe.

If it were granted to those who hold the Lamarkean hypothesis, that all the forms and forces of the *organic* creation, existing at present, originated in preceding properties of things, and in the conditions by which these properties are brought into play, this would only make the question more peculiarly pressing and pertinent—Whence the properties, and laws, and conditions of first things? If there is perspicuous evidence of design in the proportions of pristine atoms; and if, by the force and form of these, matter has been developed into the order and beauty of the present creation; then the design in the constitution of the primary constituents of things, which contemplated all future phenomena, is only the more apparent and the more wonderful.

CHAPTER IV.

EXPOSITION OF THE FACTS WHICH ESTABLISH THE DOCTRINE OF PROGRESSIVE ADVANCES IN CREATION FROM LOWER TO HIGHER SPECIES, AND THE INFERENCES AUTHORIZED BY THESE FACTS.

It is no longer necessary to elaborate the evidence of progressive steps in the exercise of creative energy upon the earth ; those evidences have long since been industriously collated. There is, probably, no one at the present time conversant with geological studies, who doubts that creative energy upon our globe has proceeded upon the principle of progress.

Exceptions to the principle of consecutive progress have been alleged at some points in the chain of organic life ; and it is true that, as the four great orders of animated beings pass from the first individuals upward, there are links where the chain is broken—but, in view of the varied and cumulative evidence which sustains the general principle, the exceptions, we think, ought not to raise a doubt in any mind in relation to successive advances in the great scheme of creation.

We do not speak now in relation to the Lamarkean hypothesis, or in relation to any hypothesis which assumes the development of one species into another by the "force of nature." Such hypotheses, if they assume that one life-property produces another, new and diverse from itself, are merely attempts to clothe natural principles with divine attributes: but still, the statements upon which such hypotheses are based, so far as they are authentic, ought not to be undervalued. Nothing is gained for the cause of Truth by impeaching a well-supported statement, because it *seems* to invalidate a conclusion which we desire to establish. There are, undoubtedly, facts sufficient to prove progress from lower to higher forms and faculties in the work of creation. There are no exceptions which invalidate the general statement that the earth's surface has been inhabited by different species of plants and animals, the most of which ceased to exist many ages before the creation of man; and that in the orders of creation each successive genus is with few, if any exceptions, higher in organization than preceding ones.

THERE ARE NO EXCEPTIONS WHICH INVALIDATE THE FACT OF PROGRESS.

The exception often referred to by able writers, that fishes of a complex structure are found in the Silurian group, may be alleged against the development hypothesis, to counteract which, more particularly, it is adduced ; but, aside from all theories, and inquiring as to the fact whether higher forms of animated life did not progressively succeed the earlier species, all parties would answer the inquiry thus propounded in the affirmative.

It is likewise true that, in the progress of ages, some species of vegetables and animals have degenerated. When the conditions of the earth's surface have changed, and certain species have continued to exist, it is found that their size usually diminishes, their number decreases, and their dominion upon the earth's surface passes away. But this obviously has been the result of changes in the condition of the globe, which were more favorable to the higher species, and consequently less favorable to those below them ; thus the higher temperature and humid atmosphere of the secondary period were succeeded by a state of the earth's surface more favorable to the conformation and instincts of other creatures, advanced beyond saurians on the scale of animated life. Hence the deterioration of lower species would be the legitimate result of the introduction of conditions suitable to advanced forms. The very fact of degeneracy in lower species as the higher came on, is, in itself, no slight testimony to the rule of progress in the process of creation.

The fact, too, that mollusks of a complex structure, and some cartilaginous fishes, existed in the early seas, is only another testimony to the well-ascertained principle that creatures were from the first adapted to the conditions of the earth's surface. The condition of the primitive seas, except perhaps in the matters of higher temperature and greater expansion, did not differ greatly from that of the seas in all ages ; hence, as marine conditions have remained in many important respects nearly the same from the first, we would expect to find, as we do find, that some species and genera of marine life have had a wider range and a more prolonged existence than the denizens of the land.

The diagram at the beginning of the volume will give a condensed illustration of the main facts, and set the order of progress in creation clearly before the mind of the reader.

The upward progress of creation, as illustrated by the diagram, is sufficiently conspicuous. We will sketch an outline to give definiteness to the impression, and in order that the reader may have in mind a distinct apprehension of the facts from which we reason.

SKETCH OF THE PHYSICAL PROGRESS OF THE EARTH.

There can be no doubt but that the mass of the foundation granite is condensed from a state of igneous fusion. The metamorphic rocks, which lie next above, are composed of masses of primitive rock, broken and comminuted into slates, which compose the schistose and sienitic groups. These rocks, laid down in the primitive seas upon the hot granitic floor of the universal ocean, bear evidence, in many regions, of being permeated, and, in some instances, changed in structure by the heat radiated from the subjacent rocks. The whole system of granites, slates, and conglomerates, are generally classed as primitive rocks. This primitive formation is called non-fossiliferous, because no traces of life are found in it. It is a fair, although not an unquestioned deduction, derived from the absolute evidences of the igneous condition of things during the primitive period, that organization was not possible in the condition of the globe at that age of time.

The hypothesis is popular that the earth is a mass of molten matter covered by an oxydized crust—that the strata of sedimentary rock lie upon the primitive as the coats of an onion, except that the one is continuous, while the rock-rinds are laid in patches of greater or less extent upon the foundation granite, which itself is contiguous to the molten matter below.

In the earliest period, when life did not exist, and when only the metamorphic or lowest sedimentary rocks had been deposited, the crust of the earth was broken and agitated by frequent convulsions. The foundation rock was not yet sufficiently thick and strong to bear up high mountain elevations; but the cracks produced were filled with basaltic and other material in an igneous state, which often in the earliest, and sometimes at later periods, overflowed and solidified upon the surface. Thus, by ejections of fluid matter from below which condensed above, and by depositions from the ocean which then covered the entire surface of the earth, the foundation formation was consolidated, upon which was to be erected the sublime superstructures of the organic kingdoms of creation.

THE GRAYWACKE OR PALEOZOIC FORMATION.—FIRST LIFE PERIOD.

When the first belt of fossiliferous rocks was laid down upon the sienites and conglomerates of the upper primitive, the seas covered almost the whole area of the earth's surface. There were, probably, some peaks of granite rising above the universal ocean. From this universal ocean, which washed and wore the rock-bed upon which it lay, the Cambrian and Silurian groups were deposited. The lower portion of this group are called the primary fossiliferous strata, because, while they were being formed at the bottom of the ocean, life first began in the waters. During this first life-period no air-breathing animals existed. Life was confined to the seas. If vegetation existed in the seas, of which there are some indications, it was in the low form of fucoids: if it existed out of the seas, it was only as rock-rust upon exposed surfaces. During this period the four great orders of animated life in the ocean began, nearly together in the order of time; but the evidence is almost conclusive that radiata, articulata, and mollusca, preceded the vertebrata. Whether the four orders of Cuvier began simultaneously or not, is not a point of importance; other criteria besides the divisions of naturalists are necessary to determine the advance of a creature upon the scale of life. Even if the first cartilaginous fishes, or plataceans, were proper vertebrates, yet no one supposes that they were as high upon the scale of life as the lowest air-breathing reptiles, which followed the order of time and the order of progress.

Professor Ansted has given one of the most recent

and accurate panoramic views of the different periods of creative energy. Of this first period he says :—" The animals we do find consist of certain sea-weeds, called graptolites—the habitation, probably, of compound creatures, which seem scarcely to deserve the name of animals ; of other polyps of somewhat higher organization, building those lasting and singular monuments, the coral reefs ; of animals removed yet another step in advance, and called crinoids ; and of a singular and extensive group of crustacean animals, known by the name of trilobites. This series of rock also include a considerable group of bivalve shells, belonging to animals of low organization, and allied to the terebratula ; a few other shells, both bivalve and univalve ; and last of all, a number of the many-chambered shells of a carnivorous animal like the cuttle-fish, a creature of high and complicated organization among the invertebrata, and which seems to have been introduced among the earliest species intended to people the primeval seas. In the older beds, at least until the termination of the first great epoch—the Silurian—there seem, indeed, only to have been introduced successive modifications and additional species of the invertebrated type ; and not till [near ?] its close did the fishes appear, as if preparing the way for the next period marked by the prevalence of more highly organized beings." *

Perfect in themselves, and teeming abundantly in the ancient seas, life is first manifested in polyps, stone-lilies, valve and chambered shells; and with these, although not among the earliest species, cartilaginous, vertebrate creatures, now classed by naturalists with placoid and ganoid fishes.† Such was animated nature during the first life-period. While we have not evidence for the statement that the creatures of this formation were successive advances from the lowest link of life, yet all agree that they formed the lowest links of the four great chains of animated nature.

* Ansted's Ancient World, c. 3.

† The classification of the ganoid fishes with the vertebrates has led some to write as if this fact militated against the absolute evidence of upward progress upon the scale of life. If no order of living beings had ever existed but the vertebrata, the evidence of a rising scale in creation would be almost as absolute as it is now. The progress from a cartilaginous, oviparous, marine creature, of the lowest species of vertebrata, to an air-breathing mammal of the highest species, surely ought to satisfy those who make most of the classifications of the naturalist. Even if the vertebra be considered the basis upon which the organization of the order is predicated, and if Professor Owen's doctrine of limbs be received, yet the new appendages, new adaptations, new and diverse physiological structures, mark a progress between the first and last vertebrate, as distinct as the difference between the articulate and the first vertebrate. But it is not the *method of progress*, but the *fact of progress* in *forms and life-forces* (as we notice in the text further on), from which we deduce evidence of the being and attributes of God.

THE CARBONIFEROUS FORMATION.—SECOND LIFE PERIOD.

The formation which succeeds the Silurian groups has been called the Carboniferous System; a name significant of the immense amount of carbonaceous material which composes its medial and upper portions. The mountain limestone and the great coal-beds are chief members of this series of strata. At the beginning of this formation, many species of things found in the Silurian and Devonian rocks perished, and are found no more upon the globe. The old red sandstone, composed of conglomerates and finer silicious material, mostly of a dark red color, lies at the bottom of the carboniferous deposits; or rather, at the transition between the Devonian and carboniferous rocks. At this point of transition between the graywackes and the carboniferous the crust of the earth was convulsed, and the seas agitated and turbulent. The conditions of the surface were greatly changed. After the deposition of the sandstone, which immediately ensued upon the breaking up of the old conditions, there was again comparative repose. The waters were impregnated with calcareous material, and the ocean again swarmed with mollusks and lime-coated creatures of various genera. They were so numerous that their exuvia, imbedded in calcareous sediment at the sea bottoms, and since elevated into dry land, form a large portion of the limestone now underlying some of the finest soils upon the globe.

Higher up in the carboniferous strata are located the vast coal-beds, found in almost every temperate region of the globe. The dry land existing at this period probably presented large areas of level or slightly undulating territory, not greatly elevated above the seas. The highest mountain chains had not yet been elevated. The alternations of fresh and salt water in estuaries and shallow basins indicate the general character of the surface. Upon the new calcareous soils, possessing, no doubt, as a component, much animal matter, grew the dense vegetation which forms the mass of the coal measures. Few vegetable species of all that composed the immense mass of bituminous coal now exist; and those few which remain, if they be really identical, are so diminished and varied that the discriminations of the naturalist alone can identify them. The vegetation at this period was luxurious and gigantic. Plants belonging to the flag and fern species grew to the altitude and diameter of trees. It was an age of weed-trees, with innumerable plants of the cactus genus as an undergrowth, and with softer coniferæ and palms interspersed.

This vegetation was probably swept from the surface into the declivities and inland lakes ; and, by a process similar to that still going on in some peat-bogs, it accumulated by aggregation and reproduction into masses, of the extent of which we can form no adequate conception. During this period, upheavals of portions of the earth's crust frequently occurred. The ocean wave, occasioned by the upheaval of lands from below, having swept the vegetation from the acclivities into the basins, would subside, and leave the accumulated vegetation covered with a coating of sediment; upon which, again, another growth of dense vegetation might be produced.

The theories of geologists respecting the formation of the coal-basins are various; some even doubt whether the bases of coal be of vegetable origin.* For the purposes of our argument, it is enough that these immense beds of fossil fuel were accumulated and preserved in the crust of the earth hundreds of ages before man was created.

During the carboniferous period traces of insects and of land animals began to appear. Fresh-water shells

* Essays on Geological Subjects, by Colonel Charles Whittlesey. Those who have observed various substances through a microscope, will probably admit that this instrument is not so much to be relied on in settling questions of this character.

were few and small. Little more is known than what is necessary to indicate that life, before confined to the ocean, had now dawned in the fresh waters and upon the uplands of the earth. New species of radiates were introduced, and a few new mollusks ; the latter species, especially of encrinites, being higher in organization than previous ones. Sauroid fishes, and some creatures approaching, if they were not perfect reptiles, exhibit themselves. Fishes belonging to genera of the previous period still exist, and some new ichthyic forms of great strength and size are found. Sauroid fishes, and many species assimilated to the shark tribe, attained at this age their highest development. Great in number and in strength, and voracious as reptiles, they held dominion as free-swimmers in the waters, while the cephalopods ruled the region below.

In the upper portion of this group, reptilian forms were first introduced. "They were not, however, members of that group through which the passage from sauroid fishes to true saurians takes place, but belonged to a higher and to a complicated type of that form. It seems clear, therefore, that while a progressive and general advance in point of organization is, in one sense, a method observed in nature, still there is not such a regular gradation that an animal of a lower organization can be supposed to be employed as the agent in introducing a higher group."*

SALIFEROUS FORMATION.—THIRD LIFE PERIOD.

At the close of the carboniferous system, convulsions occurred, which occasioned changes in the seas and in the land surface of the earth. The marks of these convulsions, intervening between the carboniferous and saliferous groups, are visible over most portions of the globe that have been examined. Upheavals of ocean beds—strong ocean currents—volcanic deposits—porphyritic dykes—twisted and overlapping strata, indicate a series of convulsions of great power and widely extended. This series of catastrophes was succeeded, as was the previous one between the Cambrian and carboniferous rocks, by a deposit of silicious material of red texture, and called the new red sandstone. Upon this sandstone, in calmer waters, the magnesian limestones were thrown down, succeeding which silicious and calcareous strata intervene up to the lias of the oolitic groups.

During the convulsions which changed the conditions of the surface at the beginning of the saliferous period, most of the species of animals which existed during

* Ancient World, c. 5.

the preceding period were destroyed. Mollusks and fishes no longer hold undisputed empire in the seas. Some species are preserved, but the forms of the survivors in most instances are changed. Species of terebratula—"the aristocracy of the seas"—maintain their place and proper persons. Nautili and fish-sharks remain, but diminished in number and in size. Life, for the most part, exhibits itself in new forms. Birds, and bactrians, and reptilians are prevalent. Land vegetation is changed. But few plants of the coal-measure species survive. The evidence is full that this was not an age of exuberant vegetation, as the previous one had been. The chief denizens of this period were enormous frogs; and some remains of birds are found, of a size and structure which partake of the marvelous.* Many of the bactrians approached the lizard in form, and the birds were probably wingless—waders and carnivorous.

OOLITIC FORMATION.—FOURTH LIFE PERIOD.

Succeeding the saliferous rocks, or rather in continuation of the same deposits,† we reach the oolitic group,

* Sir Charles Lyell's examinations in America, and the New Zealand specimens of Mr. W. Mantell, verify all that could be imagined of size and structure in *aves*.

† The saliferous and the oolitic should probably be reckoned one life period.

in which reptilian life is conspicuous in the sea, land and atmosphere. Large in dimensions, various in species, and mostly dissimilar from forms of life before or since, reptiles swam in the seas, crawled upon the land, and the pterodactyl expanded its leathern wings, and betook itself to the air. Changes of ocean and land occur at this period, but no such general destruction of species and introduction of new forms, as occurred at the beginning of the preceding formation. During the deposition of the oolites, insects appear in the air and upon the earth, and the remains of marsupialia indicate the first presence in the series of advancing life, of the lowest order of mammifers.

THE CRETACEOUS FORMATION.—FIFTH LIFE PERIOD.

Following the oolitic, we rise to the cretaceous formation. The first strata, or green sand, indicate another change in the condition of the seas. The change is most apparent over the Continent and in North America, but it is not marked by any evidences of turbulence, or of the presence of destructive catastrophes, such as appear at some preceding and succeeding eras in the earth's history. The formation above the sand is mostly cretaceous. Marine life is somewhat changed. New species of fishes appear, more assimilated to those living in the present oceans. Reptiles still exist, as in the preceding series of rocks. Some new saurians have been discovered. Encrinites, polyps, and mollusks are abundant. Traces of birds are not wanting. Zoophitæ swarmed in the oceans, and innumerable myriads of animalculæ have left their shining shields* in the cretaceous strata of England and the Continent.

TERTIARY FORMATION.—SIXTH LIFE PERIOD.

The tertiary groups lying above the cretaceous, are immediately subjacent to the drift, which marks the introduction of the present mundane period. They consist of stratified rocks, formed in limited seas and estuaries, both of salt and fresh water. They lie conformably upon the cretaceous strata, and are found covering large areas in Europe, and in the western parts of the United States.

At the commencement of the tertiary deposits extensive elevations of land took place, and some of the highest mountain chains were upheaved. Almost the entire number of living species were again changed by the convulsions which terminated the cretaceous strata, and elevated the extended land surface of the tertiary

* If the microscope has not beguiled the fancy of observers, in some cases.

deposits. Tertiary life differs for the most part from preceding species. Land and marine animals are introduced in great numbers, but they differ from preceding species about as widely as they do from present animals. Not one in twenty of the inhabitants of the seas, and scarcely any upon the land, are identical with species now living. As the tertiary deposits advance to the close of the period, the assimilation of animals to present species becomes more apparent. In the uppermost strata of the tertiary, one half of the marine animals have living analogues in the present seas, and a few species of land animals still live, which existed before the change in the earth's surface took place, which was succeeded by the present order of things.

THE DRIFT FORMATION.—SEVENTH LIFE PERIOD.

The last great change upon the earth's surface, after which succeeds the present order of things, is called the Drift Formation. It was introduced by a movement of the seas over the land, the cause of which geologists have not been able satisfactorily to determine. The general features of the formation, and the character of the force which produced it, are pretty accurately determined; but the causes which brought those forces into play are not known.

A wave or flood, loaded with masses of ice and broken rock, passed with its burden over most of the northern and temperate regions. This flood-current rose above many mountains of considerable altitude, and its direction in many cases was more or less affected by high mountain chains. Large masses of rock, torn from their beds by the power of the current, dropped at distances proportioned to their gravity. Smaller masses were worn and carried further by the wave; while the softer masses of sand and limestone were comminuted, and carried by the inundation over the hills and through the valleys of most of the known world. The lowest strata of the drift is often of a coarse material, of a breccia and conglomerate character. Above these are belts of clay; and still higher, fine sand deposits: all together indicating flood and force in the commencement, which terminated in calmer waters, quietly subsiding from the surface. During the deposition of the drift the temperature was greatly depressed. Animals existing during the last division of the tertiary period, when the drift wave overflowed the earth, were swept from the surface, and buried in estuaries and eddies, from which their remains are now exhumed and restored as the museum-wonders of a former world. But few of many species of land animals survived the drift wave. From the subsiding waters of the flood our present subsoils were deposited, lighter upon the hills, but a deeper and rich diluvium in the valleys and lower levels of the globe. Thenceforward to the present time, the water-courses and the conformation of the surface have remained steadfast, disturbed only by paroxysms of earthquake and volcanic action, which indicate that the forces still operate which have heretofore changed the surface aspect of the globe. And in reason's ear they whisper the admonition, that the tenure by which present races hold possession of the earth is not eternal.

This sketch, with the preceding table, will give distinctness to the conclusion, accepted in a general sense by all who are conversant with the subject, that the exercise of creative energy in our world is marked by the principle of progress.

It is possible that many valuable writers, in such passages as seem to deny progress on the ascending scale, mean only to protect the theistic argument against some modification of the Lamarkean hypothesis. They mean only to contest the proposition that there is a law of development, proceeding in consecutive advances *by the transmutation of one species into another.* That there is a progressive ascent from the first created forms of marine life up to the mammals of the tertiary and historic periods, no one denies.

While it is admitted that the lowest beings on the scale were as perfect in themselves as the higher ones, and their functions as well adapted to attain the particular organic ends of their being, in the conditions in which they were placed ; yet the facts which show the advance of created beings in forms and faculties are beyond all question.

It abates the strength of the evidence for the existence of God to assume that there has been no progress in the work of creation. We have often wondered at the reluctance which some excellent men have exhibited in admitting the full strength of a fact, verified by a thousand different testimonies, succeeding each other from first to last upon the theater of creation. If it could be proved that there had been no progress in form and faculties, but that vitality had flowed around in an organic circle,* an important witness for the being and perfections of God would be dead.

THE FACT OF PROGRESS BEING ESTABLISHED, THE CONCLUSION WHICH RESULTS.

If it be admitted that progress is manifest in the economy of creation, then it follows, infallibly, that

* "*Ὥστε οὐκ ἂν ἦν ἄπειρον χρόνον χάος ἢ νὺξ, ἀλλὰ τὰ αὐτὰ ἀεὶ, ἢ περιόδῳ, ἢ ἄλλως εἴπερ πρότερον ἐνέργεια δυνάμεως. εἰ δέ τὸ αὐτὸ ἀεὶ περιόδῳ δεῖ τι ἀεὶ μένειν ἐνεργοῦν.*"—*Aristotle*, *Metaph.* xii. c. 6. It may be that Aristotle does not give the fair sense of Plato in this passage.

that progress had a beginning. We do not affirm again that matter had a beginning. What we had to say on that subject was exhibited in a preceding chapter; but we say now, that a creation of finite forms and faculties, advancing from lower to higher, according to a principle of progress—such a creation must have had a beginning; and we may add, that the progress of finite material forms must have an end.

It is so manifest a truism that progress indicates a beginning, that the statement can not be argued. We can, however, define and illustrate the idea, and free it from objections.

By the statement that progress indicates a beginning, we do not mean progress in a circle, as the earth moves round the sun. Even in that case—unless matter is as old as motion, and both are eternal—a beginning might be predicated. We speak of the fact of progress in creation, as it is proved and illustrated in preceding pages. There has been progress in the conditions of our earth, and in the forms and faculties of organized beings upon the earth. This is a fact. The chain, then, may be run back indefinitely, if we can not identify the point of beginning; but, from the nature of the fact, it can not be extended infinitely. We believe that human investigation has defined the place of beginning of organic life with sufficient precision.

But if the forms of life have advanced on an ascending scale, even from a point which can not be precisely defined—if that advance has been from the first and lowest in the four orders up toward the perfect—such a scheme of progress being exhibited in the work of creation, then it is self-evident that that scheme must have had a beginning at some point in time.

This conclusion being reached, we have then a clearly-defined point of departure whence to proceed in the further process of the argument. And, at the same time, the evidence which the principle of progress itself furnishes for the existence of God is distinct and forcible. It being settled that organic forms and laws had a beginning in time and place upon the earth, then, by the constitution of the mind,* a cause adequate to the production of these effects must be assumed. And if the same agencies, the same plan, the same forces and laws, are connected with the scheme from the beginning to the end, and if it can be shown that the end of the scheme includes the intelligent and moral, then the cause that originated and advanced the series contemplated the end from the beginning, and is, therefore, an intelligent and moral cause, adequate to the production of all created things—which is the Divine Mind.

* As affirmed in chap. i. Preliminary Statement.

We will condense and repeat the conclusion :—Progress on an ascending scale must have had a beginning. If the created series are developed according to a plan, then the end must have been contemplated from the beginning. If the process of advance is characterized by unity of agency, and the end of the series by intellectual and moral qualities, then the cause of the whole economy is *one intelligent moral Power*, adequate to the production of the whole scheme of the creation : but a power possessing such attributes is God.

CHAPTER V.

ON UNITY IN THE CREATING CAUSE, AND THE EVIDENCE THAT PHYSICAL FORCES AND LAWS HAVE BEEN USED AS INSTRUMENTALITIES IN ACCOMPLISHING THE FINAL END IN THE GREAT SCHEME OF CREATION.

WE shall not endeavor to add any thing to the argument derived from the design apparent in the physical structure of living beings. This subject has been fully investigated, and the strength of the evidence, examined and cross-examined, is fairly before the world. Nor is it necessary in the present aspect of the question to expend labor upon the adaptations apparent in the structure of creatures that have perished, but which have left medals of their physical conformation in the strata of the earth. Cuvier, Owen, and their collaborators have done satisfactory service in this department of inquiry. Points connected with the mechanism of animal forms have for the most part ceased to be subjects of inquiry. The point of discussion in our own times relates more to ultimate questions, which lie back of the particular adaptations observable in animated beings.

Admitting that design is apparent in the organism of the animal creation, the question is agitated, whether the existence of the organic kingdoms of nature, and the adaptations* observable in the structure of things, may not be accounted for in some other way than by assuming the efficient agency of one intelligent moral being, adequate to the production of the phenomena—whether the inherent properties of matter and the rule of law are not sufficient to account for the production of all the phenomena which we perceive? It is difficult to give definiteness to the point of inquiry which most attracts the attention of the advocates and opponents of Theism in our own times; the preceding sentences will give its general aspect. To this aspect of the question—one which has exhibited itself as a final issue in all ages—we shall look more particularly in the current and following chapters of this book.

We have noticed the evidence derived from the dispositions of matter and the structure of animal organisms. Paley and his annotators, and more recently the Bridgewater writers, have left little to be accomplished in this field of inquiry, except to add the testimony of any new facts which may be gained by future researches. Referring the reader to these able works for details, the following paragraph will give a view of the conclusions fairly reached by researches in fossil comparative anatomy. (The same conclusions are, of course, deduced more obviously from the mechanism of living species.)

In the conclusion of Buckland's Bridgewater Treatise he says—" In all the numerous examples of design which we have selected from the various animal and vegetable remains that occur in a fossil state, there is such a never-failing identity in the fundamental principles of their construction, and such uniform adoption of analogous means to produce various ends, with so much only of departure from one common type of mechanism as was requisite to adapt each instrument to its own especial function, and to fit each species to its own peculiar place and office in the scale of created beings, that we can scarcely fail to acknowledge, in all these facts, a demonstration of the unity of the Intelligence in which such harmony originated ; and we may almost dare to assert, that neither Atheism or Polytheism would ever have found acceptance in the world, had the evidence of high intelligence and unity of design, which have been disclosed by modern discoveries in physical science, been fully made known to the authors or the abettors of systems to which they are so diametrically opposed. It is the same hand-writing that we read, the same system and contrivance that we trace; the unity of object and relation to final causes which we see maintained throughout, and constantly proclaiming the Unity of the Great Divine Original."

Leaving here, with these brief references, the evidence deduced from the mechanical conformation of things, we turn to another important division of evidence, which deduces from the *arrangement and development of a series of things* the conclusion that a supervising Power controlled the advance of the series in view of a final end. To this view of the general subject the attention of inquirers has not been so much directed. The evidence here may be so exhibited as to announce with perspicuity, and we trust with satisfactory conclusiveness, the fact that one Supreme Mind exists and reigns.

In producing this argument, that point which Buckland sets forth as the result of his reasoning in the paragraph just quoted should be distinctly observed—that is, Unity in the great governing principles of created mechanism throughout all the ages of the past. We should see distinctly that the same Intelligence has controlled in the progress of creation, developing things from lower to higher forms and conditions; and that the whole scheme, which rises from the first upward to physical and moral perfection, is a Unity. Can these two propositions, Unity in the Cause and Design in the Progress of the Creation, be established? We feel an earnest assurance that these propositions can be proved ; and we shall hope to contribute something, especially under the last head, toward reaching the conclusion. Much has already been done to demonstrate Unity of Intelligence in the Creating Cause. Design in the Progress of Creation as a single scheme—as one grand economy connected by intelligent adaptation of parts—is the direction in which we will look for clearer evidences of the existence of one Supreme Being, who designed and controls the scheme of creation.

In the outset of inquiries in the direction indicated we will notice the facts establishing the immutability and perpetuity of the laws of nature, and the proper definition of the term *law*, when used in scientific inquiries.

UNITY AND PERMANENCY OF PHYSICAL AND ORGANIC LAW.

In comparative anatomy, as Cuvier and Owen have demonstrated,* the same principles of construction have prevailed from first to last in the conformation of

* See Owen on Limbs.

the animated creation. We have seen in the synopsis introductory to these chapters, that the same chemical and electrical forces and laws have existed in all time. The atoms and the elements of matter combine with and affect each other now as they ever have done. New combinations may produce new phenomena, but all are produced in obedience to the same unchanged and unchangeable laws. The physical forces may have acted at early periods with more frequency, and the resistance being less, with more intensity ; but physical forces have affected matter according to fixed laws forever.

The physiological laws of the vegetable and animal kingdoms have continued the same. Circulation, respiration, nutrition, began with the beginning, and must continue to the end of organization. The flowerless and flowering plants, the radiata, articulata, mollusca, and vertebrata, have been multiplied indefinitely in species ; myriads have perished and multitudes survive, but both extinct and living species certify to the perpetuity and immutability of the laws which govern the whole. The same principles, adapting organized beings to each other and to natural conditions, have continued from the first. Cuvier the eminent said, " Any one who observes merely the print of a cloven hoof may conclude that it has been left by a ruminant animal, and regard the conclusion as equally certain with any other in physics or morals."

There can be no question about the fact affirmed by all science, that the laws of matter have existed since the organization or "collocation" of the physical universe—the organic laws since the commencement of organization, and specific physiological laws since the commencement of specific genera of plants and creatures upon the globe. New adaptations and new forms, rising to higher ends in the scheme of progress, have been originated, and with the new collocations and adjustments connected with new species, new laws of instinct and of adaptation were likewise originated. But these specific adaptations are all predicated in accordance with the foundation laws of structure, which were enforced when the first orders of things were created upon the earth. One cause, then, has acted from first to last in the process of creation, unless we can attribute the origin and the regulated activity of the several forces of nature to several different causes, but if there be unity in the general plan, and if all the forces and laws of nature are parts of one system, and work together in the accomplishment of a final end, then unity of causation is established, and the instrumental character of natural forces and laws is fairly deduced; because, if an intelligent process is carried to a designed end by the operation of natural forces and laws, we must either consider the laws of nature intelligent, or that there is an intelligent governor, who ordained and who controls the forces and regulates the laws of the universe.

Here, then, we introduce the main inquiry which it will be our business in this part of our treatise to investigate. *Has the progress visible in the process of creation been effected by the forces and laws of nature, as efficient and sufficient causes; or has one intelligent, controlling Power, used these as* INSTRUMENTALITIES *in accomplishing the work of progress, which ultimates in an intelligent and moral end?*

DISCRIMINATIONS IN RELATION TO THE PHRASE LAW OF NATURE.

Let us endeavor, at the outset, to get a discriminating apprehension of the importance of the phrase "laws of nature," and likewise of the points where design in the application of natural forces and the regulating rule of natural laws are to be observed. Whewell has a succinct chapter on this subject: we can do no better than to give some of its leading paragraphs, so far as they relate to the point in question, adding other discriminations which we think important.

"In the phrase 'laws of nature,' all properties* of the portions of the material world are included; all modes of action and rules of causation, according to which they operate on each other. The whole course of the material universe, therefore, is but the collective result of such laws; its movements are only the aggregate of their working. All natural occurrences in the skies and on the earth, in the organic and in the inorganic world, are determined by the relations of the elements and the action of the forces, of which the rules are thus prescribed [by law]. The relations and rules by which these occurrences are thus determined necessarily depend on *measures* of time and space, motion and force; on quantities, which are subject to numerical measurement, and capable of being connected by mathematical properties.

"It will be our business to show that the laws which really prevail in nature are, by their *form*, that is, by the nature of the connection which they establish among the quantities and properties which they regulate, remarkably adapted to the office which is assigned them; and thus offer evidence of selection, design, and goodness in the Power by which they were established. But these characters of the legislation of the universe

* To include the specific properties of things in the term "laws of nature," perplexes, if it does not mislead the inquirer.

may also be seen, in many instances, in a manner somewhat different from the selection of the law. The nature of the connection remaining the same, the *quantities* which it regulates may also, in their magnitude, bear marks of *selection* and *purpose*. For the law may be the same, while the quantities to which it applies are different.

"Now this being understood, the adaptation of a law to its purpose may appear in two ways—either in the *form of the law*, or in the amount of the magnitude which it regulates. The form of the law determines in what manner the fact shall take place; the arbitrary magnitude determines *how fast*, *how far*, *how soon*. The one gives a model, the other a measure of the phenomenon. The one draws the plan, the other the scale upon which it is to be executed. The one gives the rule, the other the rate. If either were wrongly taken, the result would be wrong too."*

These passages give some degree of perspicuity to the idea of natural law, but a more discriminating definition is still necessary. The complete conclusion of the question at issue with the Materialists can be reached only by a true definition of the term *law* of nature, as discriminated from the *properties* and *forces*

* Whewell on Gen. Physics, c. 2.

of matter. Without perfect definitions, no conclusion can ever approximate the completeness of a logical demonstration.

THE BENEFICIAL RESULTS OF DISCRIMINATING DEFINITIONS.

Since the intimation of Sir John Herschel that better definitions were needed of these terms, in order that the vagaries of the fancy might not be interposed as the deductions of accurate investigation, some advances have been made in a right direction. Mr. M'Cosh (b. ii. c. 1) has a better analysis of the whole subject, which includes the properties, forces, and laws of matter, than had been given before; and the time, we think, is hastening, when the scientific vocabulary of first things will be settled and accepted. When that time shall have come another chapter will be written by the Theists of that day, which will bring to an end the discussion between those who believe in the divinity of mind and those who believe in the divinity of matter. It will then be seen that design is apparent, not only in the adjustment of the parts of the physical universe in time, and space, and proportion, and in the *selection* of the laws which govern the changes of things; but it will likewise be seen, that new species in the organic kingdoms of nature require adjustment and regulation by law, as much as would the creation of a new globe, or the interposition of some new body in the solar system. The specific properties of a fly and its adaptation to external nature are as complex and as manifold as the properties and adaptations of a globe. It is an error which supposes that power and wisdom in the Creator is in anywise to be estimated by the magnitudes of material bodies.

It will be seen likewise, that if matter possess motion in any sense, it is a latent property—if it have a *virtus*, it is a property or quality that depends on the disposition or combination of things—that the properties of matter are developed in forces by the adjustment of one portion of matter in relation to another. The adjustment of things brings the properties into action, and the law merely expresses the mode or measure of the force.* Thus, both the forces of matter and the laws of matter depend upon the adjustment of the elements and masses of matter; *and instead of law being the cause of motion, it is its measure.*

* "The problem of inductive logic may be summed up in two questions: How to ascertain the laws of nature? and how, after having ascertained them, to follow them into their results? On the other hand, we must not suffer ourselves to imagine that this mode of statement amounts to the real analysis, or to any thing but a mere verbal transformation of the problem; for the expression, *Laws of Nature*, means nothing but the uniformities which exist among natural phenomena."—*Mill's Sys. of Logic*, b. iii. c. 4.

4

The proper analysis having been made, and definitions settled and accepted, we shall then see that the introduction of a new species into a system would derange the whole economy of nature in the region of its location, unless its new properties and instincts (if we may make such a distinction) were adjusted to all surrounding things. And even then, it may be doubtful whether, in the nature of things, a new species could be introduced and preserved, unless there were a coetaneous destruction of some old species—the introduction of new conditions, and a new adjustment of the organic families to surrounding nature and to each other. All this would be necessary, at least in the particular locality where the new life properties and forms were introduced. The animal and vegetable kingdoms of nature are a unity in particular locations, and perhaps as a general whole. They are a unity by the interlocking adaptations of one part to the other. *A hybrid can not continue, because things are not adjusted to its mixed nature.* The conditions of nature favor variety in form and feature, but resist any interposition of new properties and parts. All organized things would lose definite properties and parts, if the integrity of species could be violated—natural objects in the organic world would become a conglomeration of monstrosities; and science, in relation to the parts, processes, and laws of the organic kingdoms, could not exist. The forms of matter may change below the line of organization; but when new properties are developed into new forces, which assimilate matter into new forms, then the new individual needs to be balanced and adjusted to other organic bodies and to inorganic nature, and the wisdom and power interposed to accomplish the end is the prerogative of the Divine mind.

With this notice of the proper definition and connection of natural "properties," "forces," and "laws," and the relation of these to the introduction of new species, we will notice the evidences of the instrumental character of law and force in the process of creation. An illustration will set the subject distinctly before us:

ILLUSTRATION OF THE DIFFERENCE BETWEEN THE DEVELOPMENT THEORY AND DIVINE INTERPOSITION ACCORDING TO LAW.

The steam-engine—simple at first in its form, and adapted to few purposes—has become complex in the structure of its machinery, and varied in the application of its power. But no new mechanic forces, no new dynamic laws, have been originated; by new adjustments, and the addition of new parts adjusted to the others, designed and arranged by the mechanist, its powers have been increased, its form and movements improved, and its accomplishments greatly varied. The improvement of the engine, from the first simple mechanism of Watt up to the last noble structure placed on board an ocean steamer, has been effected by gradual development. The advance has been produced by reconstructing the machine with improved parts, and by superadding one improvement to another. The additional parts added by the designer developed the force in new directions, which were adapted to the accomplishment of new purposes. There are series of advances in different parts and processes of the mechanism, which may all be traced back as modifications and improvements of the first simple form of the machine.

Now, does it ever occur to any one that the permanent laws of things, or any of the forces of matter, would have added the new parts, diversified the forces, and improved the engine, almost to perfection, in its adaptations? The fact that the laws of matter are immutable in their nature and mathematical in their measure, renders such a supposition absurd. The final end was reached by a designing mind, so locating and adjusting matter and force in the mechanism as to advance its form, power, and adaptations, from a low to a high degree of perfection.

INTERPOSITION OF FORCE REGULATED BY LAW, A FACT IN MUNDANE PROGRESS.

But in order that our present induction may be removed from questionable premises—removed even beyond the domain of the Lamarkean hypothesis of the self-adaptation of organic forms to conditions of inorganic nature—we will confine ourselves mainly to progress in the conditions of the earth's surface, to the design manifest in the advancement of the earth from the lowest to the last mundane conditions. Whatever may be said about the question how far organized beings may adapt themselves to their circumstances, it will be admitted on all hands that the forces of nature operate upon inorganic matter in specific and determinate modes and measures. Safety and certainty throughout the universe depend upon this fact.

We shall endeavor to show that there has been progress in the physical conditions of our globe, and in the adaptation of the earth's surface to the uses of animated beings; then, if the forces of matter have been used instrumentally to accomplish by their operation an intelligent end, a Governing Mind, above and apart from the forces and laws of nature, will be made manifest.

We inquire: In the advancement of the earth from

its primitive to its present condition, have physical forces and laws been used as instrumentalities to accomplish ends in which design is clearly perceived? If an affirmative to this inquiry can be established, it will be proved that such phrases as "creation by law" can have no other import than that attached to second causes in the work of creation. In collating the facts, as we have before stated, we shall notice mainly the agency of physical forces, in order that the question concerning the adaptive proclivity of living beings may not intervene.

The disturbance of the earth's crust by igneous agency—the turbulence of the primitive seas, occasioned by disruptions and elevations from below—the first elevation of dry land, and the succeeding changes of position in land and ocean, were all effected by physical forces. This constant change in the successive conditions of the earth continued until the drift formation, which immediately preceded the appearance of man upon the globe.

Assuming, then, what no one will doubt, that all these changes have been effected by physical forces, which possess in themselves no adaptive capability, we inquire: *Have natural forces and laws been so controlled and applied as to work out a condition of things which evince the presiding agency of the Divine mind, adjusting all the changes from first to last in view of a future definite end?*

The disruptions which threw up the mountains, and elevated portions of dry land from beneath the seas, were events isolated in time and place, and *occurring without connection with each other in any physical sense whatever.* Each produced a single, separate result, which in itself could be of no value in accomplishing any intelligent design; yet the whole process produced a final result so obviously marked by designing Intelligence, that it is difficult to perceive how such testimony can be doubted or disregarded. If an end, marked by obvious indications of design, is accomplished by the interposition of blind forces, isolated in time and place, then certainly the connection in the plan and the design in the final end must inhere in a mind superior to these forces and laws.

We come now to notice a single advancing process, in which different disrupting forces and matter affected by various laws are combined in producing a common and designed result.

The elevation of one portion of the surface and the depression of another gathered the water into seas and separated the dry land. The fractures of the strata, the upheaval of hills and mountains, and the currents created by these, produced living streams of water below and above the surface. Without this varied surface aspect, and without these springs and streams of living water, the earth, or rather the universal ocean, could have been inhabited only by inferior species of living things.

Again : The agitations of the strata, the seas and the atmosphere, caused the sedimentary rocks to be laid down upon the indurated granite. Generally speaking, these rocks are softer in their texture, exhibiting stratification and cleavage, and becoming in all respects better adapted to economic uses, as they rise from lower to higher formations.

Again : The fractures and veins, especially those produced in the lower strata of rocks, are filled frequently, in primitive regions, with breccia, mingled with metallic ores. In higher series the most useful ores are deposited in sedimentary beds. Limestone and saline rock are likewise intermingled with other strata in almost every region of the globe. The ores, subsequently to their location in the different formations, have been made accessible by convulsions from below and the erosion of waters above. In the primitive regions they are located by one force; in the secondary region by a different one ; yet in all regions the necessary ores are located : so that to obtain them develops human faculties and promotes human interests; and, being obtained, they subserve ends which intelligent beings alone can appreciate and accomplish.

Again: Before many of the great upheavals had occurred, the surface was covered to a great extent with shallow seas and basins of water. These tepid waters and the moist atmosphere, undoubtedly surcharged to a greater extent than now with carbonic acid, were conditions adapted to produce in these warm basins, and upon the new, rich surface, an enormous growth of vegetation. Growing upon the acclivities, and accumulating upon itself in the shallow seas for ages, masses of vegetable matter covered vast areas of the earth's surface. This exuberant vegetation was of no value to any thing formed in connection with it, but its preservation in view of human uses was almost, or quite, a necessity. By some process, the character of which we do not now fully understand, this vegetation was accumulated and preserved from decomposition, and finally imbedded safely in the crust of the earth. Elevations and depressions of the surface, comparatively quiet in their movement (such as would not destroy but preserve the vegetable treasure), overlaid the accumulated masses with strata of rock; thus preserving in the earth, by the instrumentality of physical forces, the fuel treasure for the future man.

Again: The coal-basins are located mainly in the

temperate and colder latitudes, where a frigid atmosphere during a portion of the year requires the use of fuel. Within the tropics, where the temperature is adverse to human enterprise, and where artificial heat is scarcely needed, fossil fuel scarcely exists. Thus there are indications of a Power controlling natural forces in the conditions which produced the enormous vegetation of the coal-fields, in the location and latitude where it was accumulated, in the convulsions which covered it, and, again, in the cracks and cataclysms which produced the valleys, and exposed the fuel in the side-hills, and near the surface, accessible to human agency ; and yet all was accomplished by the agency of blind forces, isolated from each other in time and space, operating in different forms and measures, but their action controlled and their results combined so as to produce a beneficent result.

Again : What are sometimes called the economic deposits—a formation including iron-ore, coal, and limestone—receive this designation from the fact that these auxiliaries of human enterprise and industry are generally found near together ; it being almost invariably true that coal and iron, especially, are found in close proximity. The coal necessary to fuse the ores, to propel machinery, and to work metals into form, is deposited near the ore-bearing strata ; and these two are often accompanied by the limestone necessary for material where buildings and machinery need to be erected. Thus the most important deposits which the earth contains, and which, from their relations to each other for economic purposes, need to be together, are found located in the place and in the form adapted to subserve the great economic ends of human society. Although diverse as possible in their nature, each one from the others, yet the uses of the one in many regions can not be developed without the others ; hence their juxtaposition, as well as their various adaptations to develop man's faculties and to supply his wants, indicate the intelligent forecast of a designing Mind.

Again : The last catastrophe, or drift-wave, accomplished an ultimate end by combining and using the results of all previous disturbances. It fitted the earth for cultivation by laying upon its temperate regions a coating of arable soil. Soils, in order to yield a compensating return to the cultivator, must be composed of various elementary ingredients. Nothing can be produced in unmixed clay, or sand, or lime. Earths composed of all these mingled together, and containing portions of iron and particles of salts, constitute the soils best fitted for culture.* By the action of all pre-

* "I found the soil taken from a field at Sheffield Place, remarkable for producing flourishing oaks, to consist of—in 100 parts: Silex, 56; alum-

vious catastrophes the rocky strata of the different formations, especially the softer sedimentary rocks, had been broken, and their smaller fragments pulverized. By this process detritus of all the varieties of rock which the earth contains had been produced, and the soil ingredients, which needed to be mingled, lay at the bottoms of the mountains, and upon the floors of the oceans. Before the drift, soils in particular localities had been compounded, but the rocks were generally composed of constituents much more homogeneous than the drift. A final catastrophe, produced by physical forces, and wide-speading in its sweep, caused stupendous waves, probably of ocean from the polar regions, laden with ice, to pass over most of the habitable regions of the globe. By this deluge the sand, lime,

ine, 28; carbonate of lime, 3; oxide of iron, 5; vegetable matter, 4; water, 3."—*Sir H. Davy.*

Analysis of Soils from Good to Medium.—The right-hand figures are an estimate of their comparative productiveness.—*From the Rational Husbandman.*

No.	Clay.	Sand.	Carbonate of Lime.	Organic matter.	Value.
1	74	10	4	11½	100
2	81	6	4	8½	98
3	79	10	4	6¼	96
4	40	22	36	4	90
5	14	49	10	27	Grass land.
6	20	67	3	10	78
7	58	36	2	4	77
8	56	30	12	2	75

clay, and other comminuted earths and metallic oxids, were taken up, mingled together, and spread as a surface-coating of soil over the continents. In some regions silex predominated, in others alumine, in others calcium—all mingled, more or less, with iron and organic ingredients. The combined result was the production of good soils, and soils of various productive qualities. Thus the event occurred last before man which was needful to appropriate the product of previous physical, animal, and vegetable changes, and by these to fit the surface of the earth for the residence of a cultivating being, such as man.* It combined in one formation of the highest economic utility the various results of previous igneous, atmospheric, and plutonic agencies—laid on the soil covering, and thus accomplishes a *final* end necessary to fit the earth for the residence of man as a *cultivator*.

The physical causes of this last great change upon the earth's surface are still a subject of inquiry with the learned;† but whatever they were, they produced

* Among the various characteristics by which philosophers have endeavored to distinguish the *genus homo*, would not the phrase "a cultivating animal"—including the capacity to cultivate both matter and mind into better than their original conditions—mark the genus by its most essential and important characteristic?

† We believe that an old theory, much discountenanced, will yet be seen to be *natural* to the phenomena, and less in discordance with the principles of science than has been supposed.

the effect necessary to crown and close the series of changes which advanced the surface of the earth to a condition adapted to the faculties and wants of intelligent beings ; and as external nature is adapted likewise to the *moral* faculties of men,* intelligent and moral designs have both been accomplished by physical agencies. But we can not suppose that physical forces and laws can produce intelligent combinations ; hence, if design be admitted at all, the conclusion results as a logical necessity, that an intelligent Mind presides over, controls the forces, and imposes the laws of the material world.

THE CONCLUSION—INTELLIGENT ENDS HAVE BEEN ACCOMPLISHED BY THE INTERPOSITION OF PHYSICAL FORCES.

This is only an outline view, in a single case, of the advancement of the globe from a chaotic condition to an end indicating intelligent and moral design, the process being accomplished by the intervention of physical instrumentalities. The argument might be varied almost endlessly, and accumulated to any degree of strength. In the vegetable and animal kingdoms of nature the same process, working to the same final end—adaptation to the uses of man—is apparent. The human mind could not have developed its me-

* Chalmers's Nat. Theol., b. iv. c. 1, 2.

chanical appetencies if man had existed before hard timber grew upon the earth. The connection between man's capacities and wants, and the *domesticable* animals created with him, could easily be shown. We choose the single outline given, because physical forces, which have in themselves no adaptive powers, have been used to accomplish an adapted and complicated design. What has been said will give the reader an apprehension of the form and force of the argument; and further reflection, we think, will not fail to strengthen the conviction that an intelligent Mind presides over the universe, adjusts the parts of the material fabric of our world, develops their forces, regulates the operation of forces by law, and uses them as *instrumentalities*, ever working upward, and working out, by physical agencies, a plan which includes intellectual and moral ends, and which therefore proves the existence of an Intellectual and Moral Cause.*

* Cudworth apprehends the point at issue in the days of Plato, and at issue still. The present efforts of materialists, in their ablest form, is nothing else than the "Democritic fate," exhibited in the forms of modern philosophy, and in the phrases of the English language.

CHAPTER VI.

ANOTHER VIEW OF THE EVIDENCE SEEN IN THE PROGRESS OF CREATION RELATING TO THE ADAPTATION OF THINGS TO EACH OTHER, WHICH ARE NOT DEVELOPED OUT OF EACH OTHER, NOR CONNECTED WITH EACH OTHER IN TIME AND SPACE.

VIEWING the development theory as apprehended by Lamark, or by able and recent expositors of the doctrine, there are some facts which, so far as we can see, can not be made consistent with any theory of progress by the development of one thing out of another. If it can be shown that the products *natural* to certain mundane conditions were not adapted to, nor appropriated by, the things which co-existed with these products in the same series—if the floral product of certain strata is not connected with the fauna of the same series, while it is evidently connected with things existing in future and separate conditions, then the theory which affirms progress by law, without the intervention of the Divine Mind, fails in a point material to its validity. At least, all theories by which God would be ejected from the presiding control of physical forces and physical progress are proved fallacious. The theistic argument will surely gain strength if it can be shown that the organic product, and the physical dispositions of things during a certain period, were not adapted to things then existing, but were adapted to a distinctive race of beings to exist in future and separate conditions.

The tenor of the preceding paragraphs will have suggested to the reader the peculiarities of the carboniferous formation when the earth was covered with a dense vegetation, composed of succulent plants, interspersed with soft wood trees, allied to the pines and palms of low latitudes.

THE CARBONIFEROUS SERIES LOCATED ENTIRELY SEPARATE FROM MAN IN TIME AND PLACE, YET UNITED WITH HIM IN THE DESIGN.

The carboniferous system of rocks contains material that, more than that in any other formation, is adapted to subserve human purposes and exercise human faculties. There lie the limestone, the most productive iron-ores, and the coal-measures, which are almost a necessary element in human progress. Certainly no one pretends to believe that the physical features of the carboniferous series was a development of one rock stratum out of another. The old red sandstone surely did not *develop itself* into limestone, nor the coal into iron stone. Their proximity must have occurred through the interposition of a Power that can act independent of the natural connection of things in time and place.

The succession of the strata, however, is not of so much importance in the argument. The adaptation of the carboniferous strata to an end, without the formation in which they are deposited, is the main point to which we invite attention.

It is well ascertained that during the period when the vegetation which produced the coal-measures grew upon the valleys, and accumulated in the basins of the surface, few land animals existed, and those mostly of the reptilian family. There are some discriminating observers who would not assent to the statement that no land animals but reptiles existed during this period, yet no one informed upon this subject will doubt but that if herbivorous creatures existed at all, they existed in small numbers, and in but few localities. The fact is exceedingly remarkable, that during the existence of the most luxuriant flora that ever covered portions of the earth, there was no corresponding fauna to grow and multiply upon these exhaustless stores of vegetable pabulum.

Now, if this immense vegetable product had decayed, or had it been destroyed and mingled with other material, as the superabundant vegetable productions of the surface have been before and since, indications of a governing Mind, depositing in one series the material necessary for the inhabitants of another, would not have been so apparent. But this vegetation was not only produced without corresponding herbivora to consume it, but it was, as we have before noticed, preserved *safe from decomposition*, and *separate from admixture*, and locked up in the crust of the earth, whence man, who alone can appropriate it, now exhumes the hidden treasure. Nor this alone. The design is remarkably obvious in another point of view. The material of the carboniferous series is the only product of the earth upon which human progress and development are greatly dependent, which can not be produced upon the surface in sufficient abundance to supply human wants. In temperate latitudes, where human industry and advancement are secured by the greatest variety of subsidiary means—where population becomes dense owing to the productiveness of the soil and the facilities for manufactures, the vegetable fuel of the surface alone is not adequate to the purposes of human enterprise, and of man's best social condition. The fuel product of the surface must be removed in order to the purposes of cultivation; and the increase of population in any temperate region, and even in new countries recently subjected to civilization, soon exhausts the supply.* Hence, from the nature of things, human energies could not be developed in the best manner, nor the race advanced to the best social and moral position, without supplies of fuel *below the soil*, which might supply the deficiency of surface fuel. Without this deposit of fuel below the surface, human invention and industry could not have been fully stimulated, the mineral resources of the earth could not have been fully used, and mechanic arts and enterprises would have been sadly impeded.

These considerations, showing that series, widely separated in the physical progress of creation, are united in their adaptations to the wants of man, as a cultivating and manufacturing being, we hope may aid to produce conviction that the coal-mines of the carbonifer-

* As an instance of the fact here referred to, a striking illustration is presented in the rapid progress of an agricultural and manufacturing population in the United States of America. In the State of Ohio, for instance, the whole area of which was once covered with a dense forest, the timber is now becoming scarce. Where once ten dollars an acre were given for removing the wood, ten would now be given to have it restored. And if the immense coal-beds which underlie the south-eastern portion of the State did not exist, wood would soon be exhausted. In such an event, the rich and extended deposits of iron in the State could not be appropriated, manufacturing interests would be seriously damaged, and agricultural interests impaired.

ous series were designedly accumulated in view of human wants, and in adaptation to fore-determined human characteristics. Myriads of ages before man was created, this provision, made for his wants and adapted to his faculties, was located in form and place where it is needed. The provision was likewise made out of connection with the ordinary laws of animal want and supply, and the product located in a separate series from the consumer. Thus we recognize an Intelligent Mind who knew the end from the beginning, who presided over the physical and organic progress of the earth, and who adjusted things not always in relation to each other as co-existing entities; but while sometimes they are neither adjacent to each other, nor developed out of each other, they are always found in co-relation to the final end of the whole scheme.

The same adaptation is seen in the ores deposited in series of rocks anterior to the existence of man. There were no co-existing species of things whose uses were subserved by the ore-bearing strata. The exertion of power by which they were located was a useless expenditure of force, unless that power was expended in view of the future when man should exist upon the earth. The ore deposits, *in situ*, have no end in connection with organized beings if man does not appropriate them to his own uses. It may be said that metallic constituents are valuable parts of some organic structures, but this fact has no connection with the masses of ore located in veins and in sedimentary deposits. These, like the coal-measures, have supplied ingredients for soils, and thus subserved important structural purposes, while yet the immense masses of the deposits being *en masse*, are thereby of precious utility as an adapted means of human progress. In the economy of nature as a whole, these deposits are arranged as evidently in adaptation to human faculties as the eye or the ear is adapted to the ends contemplated in fitting the faculties of the body to external nature. The magnetic properties of iron, also, have uses and adaptations which human faculties alone can appreciate—uses without which the products of the earth, indigenous in different climes, could not be rendered subservient to human enterprises, or to the general benefit of the human races. Civilization would not become general, nor would all the resources of different latitudes and soils be developed, if the magnetic affinity did not exist to aid the progress of human industry and human enterprise, by guiding men in their efforts to supply the demand in one region of the earth for the productions of another. The magnetic polarity was constituted so long ago as the present form and motions of the earth were established. It was laid in the foundation, structure, and laws of the physical universe ; yet the peculiar affinity by which the needle trembles to the pole had little or no connection with the faculties or the well-being of any creature, until the progressive development of the human mind brought out its cardinal adaptations to civil divisions of the soil, and to the safe transit of the ocean.

Similar views in relation to the location of common salt, and other ingredients of early formations which find adapted uses in the animal economy of the present series, might be presented. The cases already adduced are sufficient to define the course of argument, and to authorize the statement that there are evidences in the process of creation, that things united in the final design are not always connected in development the one with the other ; but that things disparted from each other, in time and in formation, are connected in the general plan and final end : thus evidencing the control of the Supreme Being, who knows the end from the beginning, and uses natural forces and laws as instrumentalities in accomplishing the great scheme by which the earth was fitted for the residence of man.

CHAPTER VII.

DIFFICULTIES OF ANY THEORY WHICH ASSUMES CREATION BY LAW, OR THE DEVELOPMENT OF ONE SPECIES OUT OF ANOTHER.

On the supposition that creation has advanced by the development of a higher species from a preceding lower one, let us look a moment at some difficulties which intervene between the initiation and the consummation of the line of progress.

THIS THEORY MUST ASSUME THAT ALL DESIGN AND ADAPTATION IN THE ORGANIC WORLD WAS LATENT IN THE FIRST CELL.

If all organic life has been developed consecutively upward from a first nucleated cell, or from any other form of primal germ, then in that first ovum the whole organic creation was contained in embryo. Every germ contains all the characteristics which can be developed out of it. Conditions could not develop, out of the primal egg, forms the seeds of which were never in it. The seed and the power were latent there, and needed only development to exhibit in succession all the varieties of living beings. And not only this, but every primal ovum, from the first one until now, has contained a world of organic being in itself. If it be said that the egg-cell of a certain animalcule and of man are the same in form,* while the product of the one is a mote, and of the other a mammal—if the statement be designed to prove any thing in connection with the theory of development, it must be, at least, that the essential germs of higher species are still the same as those of lower or the lowest species, and that the difference of the product depends upon difference of time and upon conditions in gestation. But if all things have been developed out of one prime nucleus, then the various conditions of gestation, as well as the product of gestation, proceeded from the same nucleus. The conditions of gestation are the conditions of the parent; and the parent, with all her peculiar powers, was developed out of the pristine germ. Whether, therefore, gestation stops short with the animalcule, or advances to the product of a mammal, we see not but that, according to the theory, every cell has in it every

* "An animalcule—the volvox globator—has exactly the form of the germ, which, after passing through a long fœtal progress, becomes a complex mammifer of the highest class."—*Vest. of the History of Creation*, p. 185.

variety of life, and every variety of maternal condition. If this is not true, it is because the theory in question is not true. The theory assumes a cellular nucleus for creation, and whether primal cells be uniform or multiform—if from one all organic creation has been developed—and if external form be evidence of identity in nature, then from the cell of the volvox globator different conditions would develop all species of animated beings below man, from the globator up to man.

But further than this, and apart from conditions as means of development, there are, in the properties and substance of the cell itself, clear manifestations of design to be accounted for. If all vegetable and animal life expanded from a first nucleus, then vegetable pabulum in quantity and quality is adjusted to the animal digestive apparatus. These adjustments are various and intricate, and must have existed together in the first cell. And after the beginning, all along the line of advancing life, there are various new adjustments of sexes and other inter-animal adaptations, which occur long subsequent to the time when the ovum treasure bursts into the lowest link of life. At the points where the new sexual adjustments began, *two individuals, both different in species from their parent, and both sexually adjusted to each other, must have been developed at once ;* or the mother must have been produced from a parent different from herself, and at the same time containing in heself sexual ova, the product of which was to be different from the parent in which were developed both the mother and the ova. Now, assuming that design implies a designer, does it relieve the difficulty, or help the reason of the case in any way, to say that God, or nature, imparted these properties and laws of adaptation to the nuclei in the primal cells of things, and so constituted them, that they would remain latent until adapted conditions should develop their properties? Is not the supposition more rational, that the seeds of species were produced with the conditions that were adapted to develop and sustain the parents and the progeny?

Again: If it be granted that the chain of organic life, with all its balanced properties and numerous adjustments, proceeded upward from a nucleated cell, what law constituted and concentrated all the balanced and adjusted properties of things in that one primal granule? Nature must have gone through a synthetic process, and combined all life *in* the seed, before she began the analytic process to develop all life *from* the seed. But did it not require as much intelligence and as many interpositions of the Divine Mind to create, or even to select and adjust, the properties in the first cell, so that the various species of things could be developed out of it, as to create and adjust the same number of species at the times in which they actually began to exist? We have shown, we think, that God controlled and acted directly, in applying the forces which produced the separate and successive conditions of the earth; but if He acts directly in producing, by the instrumentality of physical forces, the material conditions necessary to sustain the different species of things, is it not a most rational analogy to suppose that the higher Divine prerogative of imparting life properties to the new species themselves was effected by a present act of Divine Power? Would not the Divine Author of both physical conditions and organic forms act as immediately in producing new species of life as in producing new conditions in which life was to be developed?

ADJUSTMENT BY DIVINE POWER NECESSARY IN ORDER TO DEVELOP LATENT PROPERTIES INTO LIFE-FORCES.

But, furthermore: If it were admitted that the organic properties of things were latent in matter, it still requires the adjustment of the different elements in which they inhere to develop these properties. Adjustment in time, place, and measure, are necessary to develop properties into specific forces, whether they be physical or life forces. The Creator, then, in the origination of each species, must make a new adjustment of things, by which the specific forces and forms of organized beings are produced; so that the new development of organic forces, and the institution of new organic laws and instincts, are a *sine quâ non* in the production of each new species which possesses distinctive characteristics.

THE DESTRUCTION OF MOST LIVING SPECIES AT SEVERAL POINTS IN CREATIVE PROGRESS NOT CONSISTENT WITH THE DEVELOPMENT THEORY.

Again: There are distinct and decisive interruptions in the line of creative advance. In two or three instances, at least, the catastrophes which shattered the fabric of the earth's crust changed the position of the sea and land, and altered the temperature from torrid to frigid degrees, destroyed almost, if not totally, the living species of things. But few living creatures survived the catastrophe which preceded the old red sandstone; and it is really doubtful whether any—if we except a few low mollusks—survived the devastating changes which affected the air, earth and sea, when the drift was deposited; yet, after the drift, the four great orders of animal life start at once into new forms. It is absolutely certain, to our own mind at least, that after this period there was no gradual development from the lower species up again to the point where the catastrophe found and destroyed preceding species. Were this the case, we should certainly find traces of development from mollusks to mammals subsequent to the drift. But instead of this, well-ascertained facts certify us that the genera of the new animal families start at points equal to, or in advance of, old forms ; and various species commence at once, and in different portions of the globe.

Now, if it be said that the new conditions were more favorable to higher forms, this undoubtedly is true ; but then, instead of developing something better out of lower forms, they would be less favorable to old existing forms, and, *according to law,* so soon as the surface-changes occurred, *degeneration,* and *not advance,* in old species, would be the results.

Besides, as former species were destroyed upon land and mostly in the waters, there were no intermediate forms for the advanced species to spring from. If one species was developed out of any other, the highest must have been developed out of the lowest, without graduated, intervening links from the lowest upward. This supposition is monstrous, and, we presume, will not be defended by any one.

These are grave difficulties in the way of the development theory. The *law is against development by law;* and the *facts* seem incompatible with this hypothesis of creation.

THE DEVELOPMENT THEORY IS PANTHEISTIC, AND GIVES AN INTELLIGENT LAW-SOUL TO ALL WORLDS.

Again: In the economy of the solar system different bodies are in different stages of progress (and this is probably true throughout the physical universe); and as it is supposed by the most recent writers friendly to the development theory, that the same general modes and faculties of life exist in other bodies which obtain in our own planet, then those life-chains must be in different stages of progress, and, consequently, there must have been different stages of beginning in different planets. There must, therefore, be several causes of beginning in different planets, or one Supreme Cause over the whole. But if the forces of nature begin to operate at different periods, and the laws of nature are only the mode and measure of the forces, how can the laws of nature, or the forces of nature, be the cause of the beginnings unless force or motion be self-caused? Whenever this class of writers, therefore, point to the forces or laws of matter, and say these were efficient in any creative act, they but renew the old pantheistic philosophy, which gives a material soul to each world, instead of a Sovereign, Intelligent Mind to the Universe—a philosophy which endows material forces with intelligence, instead of assuming an Intelligence above natural force. The old Academy, long before the era of the light which Jesus brought into the world, reached this *Ultima Thule* of the undevout reason ; and Plato, the greatest of the ancients, attained to higher knowledge, and believed in the Beautiful, True, and Good, as a supreme, self-moving, and all-moving Unity—the Parent and the President of the Universe.

THE ILLUSTRATION OF THE THEORY INCONSISTENT WITH ITS STATEMENT.

It may, perhaps, be said that these alleged difficulties, so far as they have force, are not based upon a correct statement of the theory of creation by law. We are aware that different writers present different aspects of the development theory. Our difficulties lie directly against the ablest exposition of that theory which has been given to the public in our times. The "Vestiges of the History of Creation"—to which we refer—is not, as we suppose, consistent with itself; and certainly it is not with some of the supposed phenomena by which it is illustrated. The Acarus which Mr. Crosse is said to have created by law is one of the Articulata, and was produced, it is said, immediately without passing from lower species up to its place in the life-chain of this theory. This is quite in advance of the point where they assume that the Creator began his work. If Mr. Crosse could begin with the Articulata, and create an Acarus which had no parent, why may not the Divine Power accomplish as much? If Mr. Crosse can form both germ and insect, by the same process, why may not Divine Power form both germ and mammifer? (We do not wish to be irreverent.) But how is the achievement of Mr. Crosse consistent with the foundation-principle of the theory, that the lowest species of all is the parent of all—that all succeeding species after the lowest polype are developed out of a preceding one? Is it said that the conditions fitted to the production of an Acarus were furnished? But the theory does not assume that the peculiar conditions which produced man produced him from inorganic matter, but from a preceding species; and so with other species down to the first. "Undoubtedly," says the author of the "Vestiges," "what we ordinarily see of nature is calculated to impress a conviction that each species invariably produces its like"—but—"I suggest as an hypothesis already countenanced by much that is ascertained, and likely to be further sanctioned by much that remains to be known, that *the first step was an advance under favor of peculiar conditions from the simplest forms of being to the next more complicated, and this through the medium of the ordinary process of generation."*

A GOD OF LAW BUT NOT OF LIFE.

Again: While a Creator is spoken of as a first cause of law, yet it is clearly stated, in pantheistic phrase, that this author "can not separate nature from God himself." * He finds no God in any creative act, except the first one, which occurred long anterior to the creation of life upon the earth. He finds no God in providence: All things are created, developed, and controlled by law, as the efficient agent in all terrene progress. The author *does* separate God from nature, and yet he says he "can not separate God from nature." He must then believe that God acted once, and then "fell asleep,"† or that the laws of nature were God in the beginning and law in the process of creation. It may be that this author will allow a Divine act in the

* Finding the Edinburg Reviewer speaking of the whole works of Deity as "vulgar nature," I feel that the piety which such an idea expresses to my senses is only impiety to me, who can not separate nature from God himself; but it is not necessarily so to him, whose education has given him peculiar and, as I think, erroneous conceptions of this subject.—*Seq. to Vestiges.*

† "Father fell asleep," instead of "fathers," would be a better sense of 2 Pet. iii. 4.

beginning, both of law and life ; still the main import of the book derives life from physical agencies.

THE MORAL SENSE OF THE AUTHOR RELUCTATES AGAINST THE CONSEQUENCES OF HIS THEORY.

In the last paragraph of the Explanations by the author of the "Vestiges," the moral sense and the intelligence of the writer are both apparent. After speaking in words that a fine intellect only can use, of man, his power to do and to endure, his faculties and affections, his graces and his aspirations, the thought legitimate to his theory comes out at last, and he ejaculates in relation to the subject of his thought, "Gone! lost! hushed in the stillness of a mightier death than has hitherto been thought of!" * From the thought

* At the close of the Augustan age, when eclecticism had done its best in separating the good from all systems of philosophy, still the reason, unassisted by Revelation, wandered in unsatisfied perplexity in search of one personal God, and of the greatest good. The experiences of Clement of Rome, before his mind rested upon Christ, were a counterpart to those of this author.

"I, Clement, was able to pass my first years in a moral course, since the thoughts that followed me from childhood called me off from pleasure to sorrow and exertion; for there dwelt in me—I know not whence it came—the thoughts which reminded me frequently of death, that after death I should not be, and then no one would think of me, for eternity would involve all things in oblivion. When did the world begin, and what was there before the world? Was it from eternity? Then it would last to eternity. If it was brought into existence, then also it would at of this "mightier death" the soul of the author seems to shrink, and he adds, "But yet the *faith* may not be shaken ; that that which has been endowed with the power of godlike thought, and allowed to come into communion with its Eternal Author, can not be truly lost. The vital flame which proceeded from Him at first returns to him in our perfected form at last, bearing with it all good and lovely things, and making of all the far-extending past but one intense present, glorious and everlasting." What means this—"man in communion with his Eternal Author?" Does it mean man in communion with "*law?*" According to the theory, God is not the author of man in any sense, as much as he is author of the lowest germ of animal life. "Endowed with the power of godlike thought." What means this? Reason, according to the author, is the product of material laws. Is God's thought like this? And surely, if reason is the result of organic forces, it will be lost when that organism is destroyed.

That the moral nature of the author, feeling the in-

some time perish. And what would it be again after its dissolution, unless, perhaps, the stillness of death and oblivion (that comfortless idea, which is found in several of the Oriental systems of religion, that the changing forms of individual existence will at last be dissolved into an *unconscious All*—thus universal death will be the ultimate result—all existence will become an unreal specter), and, perhaps, something may then be which now I can not conceive of."

jury inflicted upon it, has caused him to ejaculate sentences inconsistent with his cherished theory, is one of the strongest evidences that that theory is not true. After uttering the passage, "The faith may not be shaken, that that which has been endowed by the god-like power of thought, and allowed to come into communion with its Eternal Author, can not be truly lost," the author closes by giving the import of this reverent language as interpreted by his theory, "The vital flame which proceeded from Him at first returns to Him in our perfected form at last." What means this "vital flame?" Does it refer to the "fire mist," when our system first took on the rule of law, which, after having developed itself in material combinations, thence, through organic structures, finally produced the form perfect of man? or does it refer to the vitality of the first organic germ which passes through each succeeding species up to the last? This primal flame, whatever it may be, returns in the forms of all men; and not only this, but the vital chain, from first to last, returns, "making of all the far-extending past but one intense present." It is, we think, perfectly apparent that the introduction of moral conceptions into this theory is arrant nonsense, or else it makes nonsense of the theory itself.

A GOD WITHOUT INTELLIGENCE CREATED INTELLIGENCE.

But let us take another view of the difficulties of modern materialism. When it is said, "God can not be separated from nature," while at the same time He is affirmed to be "the author and sustainer of nature," the import can not be that God has exercised any personal act of creation or control since gravitation first affected the material which formed our system; or, if the theory be confined to the earth, then no creative act has been put forth by the Maker since the first organic cell was formed, and that was not formed by the Creator, but by law. God is in nature, and inseparable from nature, and sustains nature; hence the complement of natural phenomena, organic and inorganic, is all the personality which belongs to the God of this theory. Let us see the character of God as thus conceived:—

If God is inseparable from nature now, He was inseparable from nature at all periods of the past: then what follows? Why this; Reason is a product of material development: then, before the existence of organic forms, there was no reason in existence; none, at least, in anywise connected with our planet. Intelligence was developed from lower susceptibilities to higher instincts, and thence up to the human mind. Then, as a sequent of this doctrine, at early periods of creative progress by law, intelligence did not exist; and if God can not be separated from nature, before nature produced intelligence, there was no intelligent God. The highest nature in existence is the highest being belonging to the organic kingdoms at any particular period in the history of creation. During the saurian age the lizard mind was the highest in existence; and if there be nothing above and separate from nature, then the fish-lizard-god was for the time the supreme being on the earth; or, at least, the supremest being that acted in connection with the earth.

But is it said, that not only the laws and beings of this earth, but the laws and beings of our whole system are included in the idea; and that, with this enlarged conception, God can not be separated from nature. Now, admitting the conception to be expanded, then, if God can not be separated from nature, He is in different states of progress or development in different parts of the universe. God is in different stages of development in the solar system at the same time; and God and nature have together gone through different stages of development. This conclusion is the highest and best result of the hypothesis.

INSTEAD OF GOD CREATING NATURE,—NATURE CREATES GOD.

The legitimate ultimatum of this theory is, that Divine interposition being out of the question, and as the laws of nature are still developing organized beings into higher species, instead of man, as an individual returning to his Author as a vital flame, or in any other form, he will turn into something different in species from the present man. The laws of "natural development" will produce a being in advance of man; and so forward, the latter product will rise above previous ones, until *the laws of nature will create a god, instead of God creating nature.* So far as the theory is comprehensible these results are legitimate—logical products of the hypothesis of a progressive development of the creation by law.

It is a relief to turn away from the inferences and sequents connected with such theories, and seek for more satisfactory conclusions and a truer hypothesis.*

* See Excursus on Hypotheses, especially the hypothesis of *Pre-existence,* at the end of the volume.

CHAPTER VIII.

CREATION AND CONTROL BY DIVINE AGENCY.—SUSTENATION AND GOVERNMENT BY LAW.

A BETTER HYPOTHESIS.

WE propound now, as we think, a better authenticated hypothesis than that which we have been considering—one more consistent with the attributes of God, the faculties of man, and the facts of creative history.

Observing the species of fossil and living beings as they have appeared in succession, we learn that the faculties and forms of created things have advanced, not by graduation into each other, but by species specifically separated from each other in their inherent life properties, and in their relation to other things.

We place, then, an active Supreme Mind over the whole plan of progress, from the first to the last, adjusting the position of things, developing their properties, and establishing their laws. We make the whole economy of creation upon our globe one design ; then the different advances in the process are marks of creative power and wisdom, proceeding from the beginning to the final consummation. The mind which acted in the beginning contemplated the end, and worked to that end by creation, adjustment, and control, through the whole life history of the past.* The final end is the object of the first act of creation as much as of any other act in the series; and *the character of the end* contemplated from the beginning is testimony for the immutability and for the moral attributes of God.† If, millions or myriads of ages in the past, when life first began, the end in view of the Divine mind was the same which is now in process of accomplishment, then God is one and immutable. If the chain of progress

* Humboldt says in his introduction to the third volume of "Cosmos," that "while Aristotle teaches men to investigate generalities, in the particulars of perceptible unities, by the force of reflective reason, he always includes the *whole of nature*, and the internal connection, not only of forces, but also of organic forms. In his book on the parts (organs) of animals, he clearly intimates his belief that throughout all animated beings there is a scale of gradation, in which they ascend from lower to higher forms."

† "To study the succession of animals in time, and their distribution in space, is to become acquainted with the ideas of God himself. Now, if the succession of created beings on the surface of the globe is *the realization of an infinitely wise plan*, it follows that there must be a necessary relation between the races of animals and the epoch at which they appear. It is necessary, therefore, in order to comprehend creation, that we combine the study of extinct species with that of those now living, since one is the natural complement of the other."—AGASSIZ AND GOULD'S *Prin. Zoology*, chap. xiv. sec. 2.

rises from lower to higher forms, and thus reaches a final intelligent and moral consummation, then the process stands as means of accomplishment to the end, and God was the same wise and benevolent Being when saurians ruled the earth that He is now when man is monarch of the animated kingdom. All the forces of matter, and all the laws of nature, when established by Divine agency, perform their offices so long as their subjects exist. But the center of every new species of life, the new forces and adaptations which each new species exhibits, these were adjusted by Divine wisdom, and the new life-center itself was the immediate workmanship of God. We assume, then, that every new condition of the earth, from the first creation of matter and property upward, was designed and produced by Divine energy, acting by the power of natural forces, and that every species having new properties was, in its origin, an immediate product of Divine power, the whole being sustained and governed by appropriate laws.

Let us see whether the ascertained facts will not take form and relation under this statement.

PROGRESS BEGINS IN TIME.

The organic creation begins in time, and advances upward. If nature had exhibited one continued succession of like species, with only those varieties which are produced by difference of climate, then the human mind, without a revelation, might find difficulty in separating God, as a personal Being, from nature and her laws. The philosophical materialist might say, "Nature is immutable; all things have continued the same from the beginning.* Immutability is an attribute of nature, and it is likewise an attribute of God. The past and the present, both of nature and of God, are the same. Who, then, can separate God and nature, when both the natural and the Divine are changeless and eternal?" But when it is proved that change is the order of nature—not change marked by sameness, but by progress; that there has been upon our earth, and within the limits of time that may be computed, a beginning and a progress, both of the inorganic and organic realms of nature; then, unless God himself had a beginning and a process of development in nature, He is the author, and not the complement, of natural phenomena. And as the first step in the process had a design in itself, and a designed connection with the final end, then the inference is legitimate that a supreme Designer was before and above organic nature. And if there be design in first things, as well as last, and through the whole, then mind is above matter, and plan before organization.

* 2 Peter, iii. 4.

THE SUPREME BEING ACTIVE IN THE PLAN OF PROGRESS.

Then again: If God exists He is active. He is ever active as a supreme mental and moral Being. The negative of this, or the supposition that Divine agency and control ceased with the first creative act, would imply that there is no God. But if God is an ever-active Being, He would act *after* as well as *in* the first creation. But if all things had been created at once—created perfect and immutable in themselves, and thus placed under immutable laws, there would have been no possibility of Divine activity subsequent to the beginning; therefore, the first creation of things in a lower condition, from which a life-giving and a law-controlling God might advance them to higher order and beauty, and upon which, as a crowning result, an intelligent and moral system might be superinduced, would be the rational genesis of creation, deduced from the postulate that God exists, and is an ever-active supreme mind.

FORCES AND LAWS, INSTRUMENTALITIES IN DEVELOPING THE DIVINE PLAN.

Again: In order to accomplish a plan it is necessary that the designing and controlling mind should understand the *mode* and *effect* of the agencies used in accomplishing the end. It is obvious to every one that no being could accomplish a particular end without using agencies which acted in a definite form and produced definite results ; hence it follows, that *definite properties of matter*, as *second causes operating as forces under law*, would be introduced as *instrumentalities* in developing the Divine plan on the earth. A supreme mind could thus use matter in such states and measures, and apply force in such places and forms, and according to such laws, as would accomplish on earth the end contemplated from the beginning. *Reason, the supreme as well as the finite, makes rules for itself.*

ORDER OF ADVANCE BY DESTRUCTION AND CREATION.

Again : In the nature of progress to a higher end, it is obvious that succeeding created forms must be diverse from those which preceded them ; and in a series of ages of progress, commensurate with the known existence of the world, there would be almost innumerable forms of life, each succeeding genus, as a general rule, advancing beyond preceding ones. Now, when we take into the estimate the limited extent of the earth's surface, and likewise the fact that different conditions are adapted to different forms of life, it is clear that there would neither be space nor conditions to sustain, in continued existence, the myriads of species that the serial progress of creation has required : hence the march of creation through time would proceed upward by *destructions* and *new creations,* the change of conditions upon the surface destroying the preceding species, or new species destroying the older ones. In one, or in many ways, the preceding species gradually or at once, must sink from existence as the advanced forms come in ; therefore the necessities of space and conditions required that preceding species, as a general rule, should become extinct as higher forms were introduced upon the globe.

Such, in view of the facts and reasons of the case, is, in our opinion, a rational hypothesis of the Creator and the creation. Matter and its properties in the beginning ; force developed and laws instituted by the dispositions of matter ; organic life and progress from lower to higher forms ; that progress effected by the instrumentality of natural forces and laws ; advance by the destruction of lower and the introduction of higher species ; the whole produced, advanced, and controlled in accordance with a *plan* which bears the impress of a Supreme Creator and Governor of matter and mind.

CHAPTER IX.

TRANSITION FROM THE CORPOREAL TO THE SPIRITUAL.

CONCERNING WHAT WE MAY KNOW OF THE FUTURE AND OF GOD FROM THE CONSTITUTION OF THINGS VIEWED IN CONNECTION WITH THE LAW OF PROGRESS.

If the capacious and discriminating mind of Paley, without a knowledge that there was to be any future progress in creation, had deduced from the structure and habits of things existing during the secondary geological epoch, testimonies for the perfections of God, the evidence of Divine goodness would have been weak and unsatisfactory compared with that which Paley and his annotators have deduced from the present forms and fitness of things. Yet all who believe in the supremacy of the Divine mind allow that the Infinite Being, who presides over the creation now, reigned and wrought through all the periods of the earth's history. It is evident, therefore, that the created product of no single period in the earth's progress can exhibit either the best testimony or all the testimony which nature furnishes for the being and perfections of God. Any one period in the history of creative progress is but one part of a great plan which includes the whole. As that plan is developed in time, growing toward perfection with the lapse of ages, to infer the character of God from a single period in the series would be but little better than to infer the wisdom of the mechanist from the adjustment of one set of wheels in a watch, without including the scope and final end of the whole mechanism.

It is conceded, of course, that the conformation of each creature that has lived, or that now lives, is perfectly adapted to the condition and relations in which the Creator has placed it. This is a perfect but a subordinate adjustment. An individual part may be complete in itself, and at the same time be but a part of a great whole. Dr. Bell has exhibited, in a striking manner, the design according to which osseous mechanism and muscular power are adjusted in the human hand. Still the human frame, considered in the perfection of all its adjusted parts, and the whole viewed as the physical organism of an intelligent and moral being, would give plenitude and pertinency to the evidence for the Divine existence and attributes, which no one part of any created being could do. The final end of a whole plan, including the adaptations and fitness of all its parts, is the highest testimony to the character of a designer who begins the structure with its ends and uses in view.

The plan, then (perfect in itself though it may be), included in the structure of any one creature, is a subordinate and a subservient one. It may be necessary in the adjustment of a great scheme that there should be checks and balances. In a process of development there are stages and parts that are imperfect. There may be parts of a structure whose uses in themselves seem ignominious or injurious, while yet, in attaining the end of the scheme, their office and operation are profitable.*

Let us consider, then, the whole economy of creation from first to last, as one complete design, still in process of development. In a preceding chapter we endeavored to exhibit an outline of this chain of progress. Commencing with the lower forms in the great orders of animated life, we noticed the ascent, indis-

* The argument which aims to avert the conviction that malevolence is indicated by the mechanism and final end of the fang and poison-sac of the viper, and other contrivances similar in aim, are in themselves of value; but they would be strengthened and receive relief by allowing such instances of evil in the subordinate and individual subject to be classed as checks and balances necessary, not only in promoting the ends of life in the creature itself, but that the creature, its mechanism included, are adapted to work out the grand economy of a creation advancing through lower stages up to the perfect.

tinct in some of its ramifications, but obviously tending upward, until the structure is crowned by the creation of a human being, possessing an intelligent and moral nature. We noticed that it was in view of the wants and faculties of man, ages previously to his existence, that many portions of the creation had been formed and located. Let us inquire now whether there is evidence that the progress manifest in the Divine plan tends to a perfect physical and moral consummation.

When we find, by observing the processes of nature, that certain facts may be predicted of all the movements of physical bodies, or when the phenomena of life are produced continuously, according to certain methods, we call such general facts, in the order of things, laws. But when we find a method of progress which, while its advance is certain, yet the advance is by change — by interposition — not by any method mathematically regulated—then the manifest progress is attributable to a *principle* or *method* of Divine operation, and should be so designated, lest, being distinguished in no way from the laws of nature, two things which are different should be confounded as the same. But in the things which we are now to say, the discrimination is not of great importance. Whatever be the nominal designation of the method, no one will be disposed to doubt the fact.

The existence of the principle of progress, as we have shown, is certified by the history of all periods of the creation. From the beginning upward to man, progress in the general mechanism of animal forms, and in the properties of the life power, has marked the successive exertions of creative energy. Sometimes a link is lost or broken; but a sufficient number are found connected in the series to mark the place of the lost link, and to furnish indubitable evidence that there are

> "Links of life through nature creeping,
> Serial steps progressing ever."

From the lowest vertebrate the structure rises to mammals and to man. The principle rests upon data as old as creation, and data that is constantly repeated during the whole history of life upon the globe.

THE PRINCIPLE OF PROGRESS IN THE CREATION ULTIMATES IN THE PERFECT.

The principle thus ascertained is, in itself, evidence that the Divine plan covers the whole creation in all time. Not only are the different divisions of creation linked together and expanding upward, but all the different families of the vegetable and animal kingdoms are united in one plan, and adapted to each other. Each species is perfect in its place, while at the same time it is balanced and adjusted with all other things; and the principle of progress is over all. Thousands of species have ceased to be, but they were links in a chain of life, which, while it may have decayed at the bottom, it is still growing and ripening to a consummation at the top. The scheme of creation which has been in progress from the beginning covers all time, and includes all created things. Now as it is certain that progress in creation is a principle or method of the Divine operation, then, unless God has abandoned a method which has forever characterized his working, future progress is certain—progress to a consummation brighter and better than man has conceived. A consummation for the birth of which all nature has travailed from the beginning until now; and nature still travails, and the birth-throes which will bring forth a better condition of body and spirit are coming on. The creation is made "subject to vanity," or imperfection, yet we wait in hope for that birth of the perfect which will close and consummate the life-labor of the world.*

* Paul says—and if it may be interpreted in its largest sense, it is certainly an evidence of his inspiration—"For we know that the whole

The existence of a principle of progress in the creation being established, it is unwarrantable to suppose that its operation will cease until it has produced perfection. The fact that it is an established method of the Divine procedure is evidence of its stability. We may announce it as an axiom that *the will of God is realized only in the perfect.* We have proved that the perfect in creation is attained by progress. The operation of the principle, therefore, must continue, until it has accomplished a perfect result. Such a result is not attained in the present constitution of things, hence we may confidently look for a further development of the Divine plan.

PROGRESS OF EACH SPECIES IS NOT TO ANOTHER HIGHER THAN ITSELF, BUT TO PERFECTION IN ITSELF.

Apart from this legitimate and important conclusion, deduced from the history of the past and from the principles and reason of the case, there are evidences that *each series* of the creation is so framed, and the several species so related to each other, and to the laws under which they are placed, that each species, during

creation groaneth and travaileth in pain together until now. And not only they, but ourselves also, which have the first-fruits of the Spirit; even we ourselves groan within ourselves, waiting for the adoption, viz., the redemption of our body;" in a future and better condition according to the promise of Christ in 2 Pet. iii. 13.

its period on the earth, approximates perfection in form and faculty, while a general improvement goes on in the animated creation as a whole. Thus, not only the whole series of things, but each species, advances until it has fulfilled its time and conditions on earth. This is especially obvious since the creation of man and the genera of creatures which were originated with him. The advance visible in the present series of the creation is toward perfection in the proper faculties of present species, and to a complete occupancy of the conditions which the higher species fill. *The progress in each species is not toward another higher than itself, but to higher perfection in its own form and attributes.* This fact, of the veracity of which we shall adduce some instances, is a plain testimony which may be added to those we have already noticed, that if there be progress beyond the perfected species of any series, it is not by transmutation but by creation.

A brief synopsis of subjects will be sufficient to show that causes are now interworking, which will secure by their operation progress in the forms and faculties of the present species of things; and hence, when the present species have reached their limit of attainment, and filled the conditions adapted to their constitutions, an advance of condition and of created life may be expected.

CIRCUMSTANCES WHICH ARE AUXILIARY TO PROGRESS.

The stronger of each species govern the weaker ; the best variety prevails over inferior ones. The instincts of the lower animals, especially, lead them to enforce this principle. Often the stronger destroy the weaker. Now, as the stronger of each species govern, and as progeny bears the physical characteristics of paternity, then other things being equal, present species will continually improve.

As in former periods of the creation so in the present, individual species—as the Dodo—have ceased to exist. Having accomplished the end of their being, in connection with the great scheme of the Creator, they sink out of the life-chain.

Man, the last production of creative energy, is the enemy of all destructive and poison-bearing things. If man, therefore, with his present facilities to destroy, shall fully occupy the habitable parts of the globe, injurious species of animals will be subdued or destroyed.

Thus, not only do species improve and injurious species diminish, but, by the laws of nature, the qualities of manhood will likewise advance. Individuals from families, that are enfeebled by luxury, or by want of exercise in the open air, or by hereditary disease, are less prolific than the active, healthy parent; and the children they do beget are less likely to live and beget others. Thus the weak by indulgence or disease recede, while the better in corporeity advance.

The mingling of races improves the human constitution in the general issue. On the American continent an admixture of blood, such as the history of man never furnished before, is in progress. "All kindreds, and nations, and tongues, under the whole heavens," are to mingle in the new world, and work out a final result in the physical, mental, and moral condition of humanity, as perfect as the present constitution of things will allow.*

The laws of health and happiness are better understood by each succeeding generation.† In the present

* Is it not true, likewise, that wars, when they are prompted by power and not by patriotism, draw mostly from the lowest and worst of the human family:—thus bad seed is destroyed.

† Macauley tells us that "the term of human life has been lengthened in the whole kingdom of Great Britain, and especially in the towns. In the year 1685, not accounted a sickly year, more than one in twenty of the inhabitants of the capital died; at present, only one in forty dies annually. The difference between London of the nineteenth century and the London of the seventeenth century is greater than the difference between London in ordinary years and London in the cholera."

M. Charles Dupin, in a recent paper read before the Institute, says that "from 1776 to 1843 (sixty-seven years), the duration of life had been increasing in France at the average rate of fifty-two days annually, so that the total gain in two thirds of a century amounted to nine and a half years; and that in no year of that period, whether during the Republic, state of civilization all the experiences of the past are accumulated, classified, and improved, in the present; and with present means of intercommunication, and the influence of the printing press, retrogression is impossible—advance certain.

Many other items might be added—these are sufficient to show that the power of progress is still operating by improvement of species, and by extinction of some species, and the numerical increase of better ones; and hence, by analogy, when the present races have reached their limit in form and condition, a general change of conditions will again ensue upon our globe.

If, therefore, we consider the present imperfect state of the creation—that the Divine attributes seek perfection as an end, but that the present physical constitution of things will not admit of ultimate general perfection in the present series; * and consider in connec-

the Consulate, or the Empire, did the annual increase fall below nineteen days."

* It may be said in abatement of the anticipation of future good, that, under the permanent laws and relations of the solar system, only a certain degree of physical perfectibility is attainable upon our planet. But if the present physical *condition of things upon the earth* be not ultimate, as we have every reason to believe that it is not, then, without affecting any *law of the solar system*, the constituents of the atmosphere—the relations of light, heat—the magnetic and other occult principles, and especially the igneous dissolution and re-construction of the mundane fabric—may, by new adjustments, produce new conditions, which will sustain physical good and restrain physical evil.

tion with this the fact that progress toward perfection is a principle of Divine procedure, the operation of which still continues; the advance of creation to the perfect will be put, we think, beyond question. The principle itself, and the attributes of the Creator, assure us of the final result.*

THE MORAL PERFECT THE END OF CREATION.

There are yet other and higher considerations, of a moral character, which indicate that beyond the imperfect present there is a perfect future. The fact, as

* "The doctrine of a life to come, some persons will say, is a doctrine of natural religion; and can never, therefore, be properly alleged to show the importance of revelation. They judge perhaps from the *frame of the world*, that the present *system is imperfect; they see designs in it, not yet completed; and they have grounds for expecting another state, in which these designs shall be further carried on, and brought to a conclusion worthy of infinite wisdom.* I am not concerned to dispute the justness of this reasoning; nor do I wish to dispute it."—T. BALGUY, D.D., *Discourse.*

So Bishop Butler, in his sermon upon Human Ignorance, says in a note:

"Suppose some very complicated piece of work, some system or constitution, formed for some general end, to which each of the parts had a reference; *the perfection or justness of this work or constitution would consist in the reference and respect which the several parts have to the general design.* Or a part may have this distant reference to the general design, and may also contribute immediately to it. For instance: if the general design or end, for which the complicated frame of nature was brought into being, is happiness; whatever affords present satisfaction, and likewise tends to carry on the course of things, hath this double respect to the general design."

we have stated, that the present condition of things is imperfect, and that further advances is possible, indicate that the Divine plan has not reached its fruition. This is clearly perceived when we consider man as the crown of the present creation, and his intellectual and moral faculties as the latest and highest product of Creative Power.

We have dwelt upon the advance in animal structures and faculties. We turn now to the intellectual and moral nature of man—to attributes which place man supreme over the creatures and assimilate him to God, having the knowledge of good and evil. The preceding processes of creation close with the introduction of a moral nature. Creation has been developed upon a material basis up toward *moral* perfection. Corporeal natures have been lost—species and genera of mere animals have ceased to be. This indicates that the corporeal and animal structure of things is subservient to the moral, as means are subservient to a higher end. *The ultimate aim of the principle of progress is perfection of moral attributes ; and to this the corporeal organization of all things, from the dawn of creation, has been auxiliary.* In the nature of man we find evidence both of a perfect future, and of the being and attributes of God. Let us notice these in order. First, what the nature of man reveals concerning a future better than the present; and second, what it reveals concerning the moral perfections of God.

PREVISIONS OF THE PERFECT IN MAN.

There are in the soul of man previsions of the perfect. The mind can, and the poet does, create scenes of beauty, of love, of sublimity, far beyond the present condition of things.* If the pure-hearted poet had the power, he would actualize upon earth a condition of things where sweetness of affection, beauty of nature, might of intellect, and majesty of morals, would combine, as they never can in the present earth. The mind of man can in its present state create this ideal world of well-being and beauty, and people it with perfect and happy beings. This, certainly may be taken

* Is man a microcosm? Do the best minds contain in themselves types of the past and future? It would seem, at least, from some passages in authors of the highest style of genius, that scenes unknown to them, both in the past and future, were mirrored in the magic glass of their consciousness. Perhaps no man is able now to describe a scene, and the most singular creature of the saurian age, better than Milton has done it. Geology had not revealed the fact in Milton's day, that such a creature as the Pterodactyle ever existed. Now we have the restored osseous structure, but who can give a more graphic description than the following?—

"The fiend
O'er *bog* or *steep*, through *strait*, *rough*, *dense* or *rare*,
With *head*, *hands*, *wings*, or *feet*, pursues his way;
And *swims*, or *sinks*, or *wades*, or *creeps*, or *flies*."
Par. Lost, b. vii.

as an indication that there will be such a condition, and that the soul of man is created capable of becoming a denizen of a better state. If no such condition can be realized or attained in the future, the nature of man is a sophism, because it foreshadows a future condition which is yet never to be attained.

MAN CAPABLE OF APPRECIATING THE MORAL PERFECT.

There is likewise a capability in man to appreciate moral excellence in advance of present attainment. Men often admire in others what they are unwilling to be themselves. "Bad as the world is, respect is always paid to virtue." Self-sacrifice for the good of others, or for the cause of virtue, has been canonized in all ages. Even among pagan nations, where the moral faculties are perverted by a false credence, the nature of man has spontaneously testified that there is in humanity a capability to appreciate the true and the good. Visions of a future good beyond the present condition have been the indigenous product of the human mind in all ages. These visions, shaded by the colors of the peculiar theology of every people, have been consecrated by the human races as a part of a good man's inheritance in the future life. Man produces from himself a moral future better than the present; and if he conceive of evil in the future, it is only as the penalty of sin, indicating that a sense of justice, as well as of mercy, are mingled in his visions of the future state.

SENSE OF THE PRESENT IMPERFECT IN MAN.

There is likewise a consciousness in many men of the imperfections of the present state. Perhaps this is true of all men. A sense of the present imperfect moral condition of the human soul, and aspirations for a higher good have been expressed by deep thinkers in every age of the world. Grotius has collected many passages, in which the mingled convictions and aspirations of the old Greeks and Romans come out in the heart-utterances which they have put upon record.*

* Araspes the Persian, in order to excuse his treasonable designs, says: "Certainly I must have two souls, for plainly it is not one and the same that is both evil and good; and at the same time wishes to do a thing and not to do it. Plainly, then, there are two souls; and when the good one prevails then it does good, and when the evil one prevails then it does evil."—Zen. *Cyrop.* vi. 1.

"He that sins, does not do what he would; but what he would not, that he does."—Epictetus, *En.* ii, 26.

So Ovid (*Meta.* vi. 19), in language used almost verbatim by the apostle Paul:—

"aliudque Cupido,
Mens aliud suadet. Video meliora, proboque;
Deteriora sequor."

Desire prompts to one thing, but reason persuades to another. I see the good and approve it and yet I pursue the wrong.

THE SOUL OF MAN CAPABLE OF MORAL CULTURE IN VIEW OF THE PERFECT.

Another indication that a perfect moral future is a part of the Divine design, is seen in the fact that man is so constituted that his best condition in this life is realized by living under the influence of that faith which affirms a future moral state, purer and better than the present. Man attains his highest moral condition in this world by a faith which produces love and reverence for a pure Being who inhabits eternity; by hopes which aspire after a higher perfection, and by a sense of responsibility which connects the trials and duties of the present state with the awards and employments of the world to come. Upon the supposition that God is a benevolent being, the thought can not be entertained that he would predicate man's best moral condition on earth upon hopes and convictions which are never to be realized.

This thought is more obvious when we consider the present life as a state of probation or moral culture. We know it is true, not only from revelation but by experience, that confidence in a better state to come renders the trials and conflicts which men bear in this world a blessing to those who endure the discipline in view of a future life. The blessings which spring from earthly trials are grounded upon faith in God's character, in connection with a future life. Without faith in the future, evil in this world can not become a blessing. Can we suppose, then, that the moral world is so constituted that evil is turned to good by that which is not true?

MAN ACTUALLY IN PROBATION UNDER THE INFLUENCE OF CULTURE.

The character of influences about us will, by thoughtful consideration, admonish every one that this is a state of probation or moral trial. All are subjected in the present condition to temptations adapted to seduce to evil, or to suasion which induces to good. Within the limit of every man's observation are good and bad examples—good and bad books. Every man's heart is open, and every man feels the power of good and evil influence. Man is conscious of good monition and of evil suggestion in himself; and it is a law of nature that the exercise of our moral powers under evil suggestion or influence, confirms evil habits and an evil disposition; and so on the contrary, when men's moral faculties are exercised in obedience to good influence, a good character is formed. The present life, in the present condition of things, is, therefore, a state of moral formation. This is not only true of each individual, but the progress of the whole, taking the sum of individuals and of generations in time, indicates that moral culture is advancing, and that the family of man, as a whole, are rising in the scale of moral excellence.*

Now, then, as human trials can only become a blessing by faith in the future—and as man as an individual, and man as a genus, is advancing in good, and to good, by convictions which realize a better life hereafter, who shall say that God has constituted man, individually and socially, so that his best good arises from fallacious conceptions? But if the convictions which produce man's best condition be true, then there is a future and better state for those whose culture is adapting their character to the condition hoped for.

* No one can study human history without perceiving in the progress of society what we see in the geological advances of our earth—disruptions of human society; certain nations and classes of men attaining the highest state which their fundamental convictions would allow. Streams, and sometimes disrupting floods of population, set in various directions—new strata of society are formed over large areas—the old disintegrated masses are formed in with the new; and yet, amid all those changes of location, of condition, and of opinion, it is easy to see the Divine Providence over all, shaping all social disruptions and formations so as to secure in the issue a general advance of the civil, social, and moral interests of men. There are, of course, in time and place, local advances and reactions; but a general advance is the certain issue of the whole. A recent writer has developed some of the principles by which the final advance from our period forward will be secured. It is the wisdom of the statesman and the glory of the church to give the principles of progression proper applications.—Vide *The. of Hum. Progression.*

THE SOUL OF MAN MAY RECEIVE A CULTURE HERE WHICH RAISES IT SUPERIOR TO THE BODY AND ITS TEMPORAL SURROUNDINGS.

Again: The soul of man can be elevated by culture to moral attainments beyond his present circumstances, or to a condition which renders his present temporal surroundings unfitted to his spiritual attainments. He can be cultivated until he becomes superior to the condition in which he is placed. He can follow light and cherish love until he draws from the objects of the spiritual world good beyond that which he can gain from earthly things. As a matter of fact, there is in the world a faith by which the "substance of things hoped for" *is* drawn from "the evidence of things not seen." Whether men account the Christian Record a fable or a fact, still the statement will not be questioned, that those who believe it may draw from the manifestation of love and purity in the New Testament a soul-culture and a spiritual benediction, beyond what all the treasures of earth can yield. Such being the nature of man, *if the Christian Religion be not now a revelation from God, God ought to reveal it; because the spiritual appetencies of humanity demand the spiritual pabulum which it furnishes.* And as man is raised above his present condition by faith in a better world and a better future, it is due to man's moral constitution that such a future shall exist.

BY THE REVEALED CHARACTER OF GOD, MEN ARE ACTUALLY CULTURED HERE INTO FITNESS FOR A BETTER LIFE THAN THE PRESENT.

Furthermore: Man is created capable of knowing and appreciating the attributes of a Divine Being, whose perfections are beyond the character of God, as that character is revealed in the present constitution of things. Now (as we shall show more fully hereafter) the character of God is the rational and only means of moral culture; and if man can apprehend and appreciate a Divine Being, perfect beyond what the present condition of nature reveals, and if this character is *revealed,* we may infer that it is the design of the Maker that man, in his present imperfect state, should be cultivated into a moral character, which will fit him for a condition in advance of the present. In the love-sacrifice of Christ, as we shall see, there is a manifestation of benevolence above that which can be learned from all that man can know of created things. Man can appreciate and aspire to this supermundane excellence; and in the case of every one who possesses true faith (faith that moves the heart and will in accordance and in consistency with the character of the things believed), the manifestation of God, given to man in the present state, elevates him to the character required by the future and better state. Thus, conformity to the character of God revealed in Christ is conformity to the character of God ruling in a better state than the present ; a conformity which lifts the soul above the condition and surroundings in which it now exists, and above the qualities and natural propensities of the present corporeity. It is thus fitted for the new creation to which it aspires in a better life. Unless, therefore, God fit men for a condition which shall never ensue, there is a better life—a life of perfection beyond the imperfect present.

Through the influence, then, of agencies at present existing, the soul may be elevated above its present corporeal vehicle, and raised out of affinity with the physical and moral condition of things in which it is placed. Men may, and some do, attain a spiritual state in this world, which demands, according to the laws of adaptation, a better physical organization—fitted to be the instrument of a mind which has been cultured into a better spiritual condition than the one natural to the genus.*

* "That which is born of the flesh, is flesh; and that which is born of the Spirit, is spirit."—*St. John*, iii. 6. *Philippians*, iii. 20, 21.

GERMS OF A FUTURE AND BETTER LIFE PERCEPTIBLE IN THE SPIRITUAL CONSTITUTION OF GOOD MEN.

It is well known to naturalists that Swammerdam, by a process not necessary to detail here, discovered the lineaments of the butterfly in the caterpillar, even before its metamorphosis into a chrysalis.

This fact has its analogy in the spiritual economy of all *good* men.* We say, all *good* men, because it is true that there are many of the human family who possess an *inoperative* instinct of immortality, but in whose bosoms no spiritual insight can discover the *lineaments* of a future life. We use the analogy, therefore, only so far as it goes. But have we not in this analogy, viewed in the light of Swammerdam's discovery, a distinct intimation of the *anastasis* of those individuals of the human family in whose bosoms are found the germs of a life, the intuitions and habitudes of which differ from those of the present existence.

The statement can not be questioned, that in the bosoms of those who are truly Christians there exist the germs and lineaments of angelic life. A new and distinct class of affections, hopes, and aspirations exist;

* It was ascertained by Raumer that an injury inflicted upon the chrysalis produces a defect in the future fly. And those who have observed know that in many species the greater number of nymphæ *utterly perish in their own pupæ.*

or rather, the affections and asperations are detached measurably from earthly objects, and exercised upon new objects of life and love.

The manner in which the lineaments of the butterfly are attached to, or detached from, the body of the caterpillar, is a process which can not be observed; neither can we discriminate in regard to the attachment to, and detachment of, the new life from our earthly hearts and habits: but one exists as really as the other. New appetites are developed, which are satisfied only with spiritual things. The conscience recognizes new obligations, which are of a spiritual character. There are new hopes and fears, and a new direction of the will. So that, as a matter of fact, the moral powers of the soul are becoming detached from earthly things as their supreme good, while they are simultaneously developing themselves into the form and features of a new life.

THE MORAL CHARACTER OF GOD IS PLEDGED FOR THE FUTURE AND BETTER LIFE OF GOOD MEN.

There is another induction in this argument which connects it with the moral character of God, and to a mind possessed of moral culture it will have a high degree of conclusiveness. The constitutional instinct which God gives to the insect becomes operative in *the insect itself*, and secures for it the future metamorphosis. The instinct in the animal leads it to a preparation for the future life, and the constitutional instinct given by the Creator verifies his truthfulness by the result which ensues.

The earth-born worm, which weaves for itself a winding-sheet, bids farewell to its present constitution and instincts, and enters a chrysalis as its grave, can not be supposed to have more knowledge than man, in the same circumstances, of the process of transmutation which issues in a new life. The two facts are palpable. God gives the instinct, and God vouchsafes the result of the preparation produced by that instinct.

Now, in men is found this instinct of a future life, and in good men it becomes operative. It assumes the forms of hope, aspiration, and volition, which actuate them to a preparation for life beyond the grave. And if men do not regard during life the instinct of preparation for the future life, then, if they approach death in a state of sanity, conscience unfailingly charges them with a neglect or betrayal of their spiritual interests.

Now associate these facts. The instinct of a future life actually exists in man. It leads good men to prepare for life beyond the grave. In the bosoms of good men are found distinct and clearly-defined elements of the angelic constitution; that is, life cherished by love, and exercised upon spiritual objects. Then, as God does not disappoint the instinct where it has been operative in the lowest of his creatures, but crowns the preparation with fruition in a higher life, can we suppose that a constitutional conviction, producing alike preparation in *good men,* will not terminate in like manner? Will not the Maker verify the conviction begotten by himself, and upon which his highest earthly creatures have acted? "GOD IS TRUE;" and our faith may rise to assurance that the good man's mortal life terminates at the commencement of an existence of "joy unspeakable and full of glory."

OUR CONCLUSION AUTHORIZED BY THE SACRED SCRIPTURES.

This conclusion, we think, is verified by the teaching of the Christian Scriptures. The tone and tenor of the New Testament on this subject have not been fully appreciated; perhaps not fully understood. The "crucifixion of the flesh;" the "putting on of the new man;" the "groaning" in the present condition to which nature is subject:—what mean these and similar inspired utterances in the Scriptures? What is the import of the apostle's word, when he says that he accounts all temporal things but loss, and struggles "if by any means he may attain to the resurrection of the dead?" Did he not seek, with intelligent aim, that moral condition in which the appetencies of the soul would demand a resurrection body, more perfect than the present, and adapted to accomplish the will of the soul in the higher moral condition to which the apostle hoped to attain? The preceding passages, and those of similar import in the New Testament, certainly sustain the conclusion to which our course of thought upon the processes and analogy of nature has brought us.

We have no data to determine accurately the period of the consummation. Neither prophetic symbols nor natural indices can direct us to a specific period in the future. Centuries may yet be consumed in the process; but still the fact, we think, is indubitable, that man is exhausting the material* and filling the capacities of his present limited condition, and advancing slowly, but certainly, to the ultimatum of his development in the present state. This being attained at some un-

* Calculations have been made to show that the coal-fields of Great Britain will not last forever, and there are certainly sufficient data to apprise us that the foundations of British commercial ascendency will be seriously *undermined* in some most important localities, at a period not incalculably distant. In the United States the supply may seem inexhaustible; but the extraordinary demand and consumption which will ensue ere long will cause a reduction of the product of American coal-fields, the rapidity of which can not now be imagined.

known point in the coming future, the final end of the present constitution of things is gained, and the catastrophe which is to change the present into a higher material and spiritual economy will surely ensue. "We, therefore, according to his promise, look for new heavens and a new earth, wherein dwelleth righteousness." *

GOD AS REVEALED BY THE PERFECT MORAL FUTURE WHICH IS YET TO BE.

Having noticed the indications seen in the nature of man, which point to moral progress in the future, we close with a brief reference to a cognate subject—*indications of the being and attributes of God,* seen in the human mind.

In the nature of man we reach the apex of a column, from which the being and moral excellence of the Creator are distinctly perceptible. It is not necessary to re-write in this place what has already been said so ably by the great masters in natural theology. It has been made plain that the moral nature of man furnishes the most clear and satisfactory evidence of the

* 2 Peter, iii. 13. See also Chalmer's sermon on the New Heavens and the New Earth. We argue for the import of this phrase, whether the future perfect be attained on the present globe or elsewhere.

The Scriptures teach that the soul will survive, and the earth will survive, but that the body of both will be *changed* or new-created.

moral character of God. Man in his present state, considered in his *capabilities rather than his character*, vindicates the moral character of the Creator, both in the past and present. Before man was created, the phenomena of nature furnished scarcely any evidence of the moral attributes of the Divine Being. But in the capabilities of man's nature when properly cultured, and in the perfection to which the moral creation is tending, we may see the Creator clothed in the glory of his moral attributes:—The supremacy of conscience, the fact that the highest good of man is found in love to God as supreme, and to man as a brother; the fact that spiritual peace and blessing are connected with benevolent exercises, while unrest and evil are the concomitants of malevolence; the fact that right loving produces as a sequent right living; and that these, being declared by revelation, are now known by experience to be the conditions of man's chief good; the great fact that man's greatest good as a being arises from moral goodness in exercise—assure us, beyond a doubt, that the Maker possesses in perfection the moral goodness in which man, as a creature, can alone find his chief end.

The mind of the designer certainly includes the idea of the whole design, from the beginning to the end. There is in every plan originated by Intelligence a connection between all the parts and the final end of the whole. The process of creation is merely the carrying out in time the divine idea existing from the beginning; hence the moral nature of man, in its perfection, was from the beginning in the Divine Mind.

We have seen that the principles of progress, verified by all the past, and the moral character of God, as that character is exhibited, especially in his last and highest creature upon earth, affirm the perfection of humanity in the time to come. We may assume, then, that end as accomplished in the resurrection, and predicate a perfect man as the creation of God; then looking at the perfect being which will crown, as a final result, the work of creation, we learn glorious things concerning the great Author:—humanity is perfected; man is a "living soul" united with a perfect body, which is adapted to actualize all the volitions of a perfect mind. The reason perceives the true relations of things. Conscience is enthroned. The affections are pure and influence the will. The Highest and Best Being is loved supremely, and finite beings impartially. The physical conditions of the earth harmonize with the perfect in its inhabitants. The law of progress is fulfilled—God's attributes are vindicated—the moral finite is perfect on the perfect earth, and the moral infinite is perfect over all.

In such a creation, which the law of progress, the character of man, and the character of God, assure us is to be, the attributes of the Infinite One will be reflected as from a mirror. The mind of the perfect man will be conscious of the Divine impression upon the disc of his soul. Perfected nature will proclaim by a voice, sounding from the beginning on to the final end —GOD EXISTS; SUPREME, AND WISE, AND GOOD!

BOOK TWO.

OF MAN AND HIS RESPONSIBILITIES,

CONSIDERED IN CONNECTION WITH

DIVINE LAW AND DIVINE REVELATION.

LAW AND LOVE ARE ONE IN GOD.

THE AUTHOR.

INTRODUCTION.

It is scarcely possible for men to separate the outward exhibition of Christianity which they see about them from New Testament Christianity, as it is revealed in the life and teachings of the Christ and his apostles. It is a first and natural bias of the mind to conclude that the prevalent conduct and character of professors of religion give a correct impression of the *spirit* and *practice* required by the Gospel.

When we remember, too, that some of our own dearest friends, in whom we have the utmost confidence, and with them many of the best men of our times, are enrolled as disciples of Christ, in some Christian denomination, our impulse to take the Churches of our times—especially those Churches in which we have most confidence—as the exponents of true Christian practice, becomes strong and decisive. Many inquirers for truth—especially skeptical inquirers—often forget what they should always remember, that the best Christians are often conscious of falling below the spirit and self-denying life required by the Redeemer, and that the mass of the professing world is as darkness compared with the Gospel light.

Now, because of the conviction before mentioned,

when evidence has been adduced which leads a man to inquire seriously concerning the Divine authority of the Christian religion, he naturally turns to the Churches, and seeks in them an illustration of the principles and practice which the Gospel requires, and his decision concerning the truth of Christianity is often influenced decisively by the imperfect lives of Christian professors. These he takes as an exponent of the Christian system, instead of that active benevolence and exalted purity which would be the true product of perfect conformity to the example of Christ.

It will be readily perceived, therefore, that just so far as the principles and practice of the Churches are not conformed to the teachings of the Gospel, the man who takes these as an illustration of what the Gospel is, will have his convictions of the nature of true religion perplexed and perverted. This would be especially true in minds not conversant with the Holy Scriptures. Hence, in Papal countries, a corrupt Church repels the reason by claiming to be the representative of Divine Truth; and thus infidelity becomes prevalent, and skepticism is in one sense true to reason, while it rejects as falsehood the religion of the State. And hence in all countries, Protestant or Papal, those claiming to be disciples of Christ, whether they be teachers or laymen, who "come to be ministered unto and not to minister," exert an evil influence upon inquiring minds.

Is it too much to say, that while we are sure that the best men in all ages have been made so by faith in Christ, and while the truly good men of our own age are undoubtedly found among professing Christians;

yet, if an angel who understood the New Testament were to look upon the earth for the first time, he would scarcely conceive that many of the Church forms, and Church offenses against the plain Scriptures, which are prevalent in our own times, could be predicated upon the simple, self-denying doctrines and practice inculcated in the Gospel of Jesus of Nazareth?

We shall reach in the next paragraph an aspect of the subject which will relieve our minds from any painful sensations which these discriminations may have produced. We make them because we are anxious that the reader of this volume should look at the "excellency of the glory of God, as it is revealed in the face of Jesus Christ," and not have his conceptions of truth and duty perverted by the imperfect exhibitions of Christian character which he sees about him. Our book does not aim to establish the fact that the God revealed in any particular church creed is perfect, nor that the Christianity exhibited by the worldly churches of our times is divine. We affirm, and shall prove, that *the God revealed in Christ is perfect*, and that *the Christianity of the New Testament is divine.*

When rightly considered, the imperfections of human practice under the Gospel would lead inquiring men to a very different conclusion from that at which they usually arrive. It is one of the best evidences of the purity and power of our holy religion, that its teachings are still so far in advance of the conceptions and practice of the world, and even of the greater number of its professed friends. The Gospel came to the earth in an age of intellectual light, but of great moral deterioration; and the inspired apostles were not all in their graves before its pure doctrines were perverted by the sophisms, and its practice corrupted by the bad principles of some of those who professed to receive and teach its heavenly truths. The fact that men fell below the pure conceptions of the Gospel the moment that inspiration ceased, is certainly a striking evidence of its heaven-born purity. And the additional fact that the vital power of the Gospel in the souls of men has increased from the time that the Bible was unvailed during the Reformation, up to our own times, and that the pure Scriptures still continue to dispel the darkness which began to gather upon them at the death of the apostles, is a testimony which produces assurance that there is inherent divinity in the Christian Revelation, and that, empowered by the Divine presence and agency, it will, in the end, work out the great process which will "bring glory to God in the highest, on earth, peace, and good will to men."

Leaving, then, the imperfect example of professing Christians, learned questions about the Jewish Hagiographa, and other things which do not relate to the sanctifying central truths of the Gospel, to be discussed by others, and remembering that inane or dogmatic disquisitions about the Gospel is not the Gospel, let the reader turn away his mind in charity from what he may deem unreasonable, unscriptural, or selfish in the opinions or practice of the churches, and examine with me the question of the Divine authority of the Gospel upon its own merits and adaptations.

CHAPTER I.

EXPOSITION OF THE NECESSITY AND RULE OF LAW.

God governs all things by laws appropriate to their respective natures. The laws which govern physical phenomena are written in treatises on the different branches of natural philosophy. These have been referred to in the preceding book. Mental and ethical philosophy relate to the laws of man's intellectual and moral constitution; and although definitions are not settled in this department of study, yet valuable attainments have been made in the knowledge of the laws which govern in the mental and moral departments of the creation. If there be any province of nature concerning which we know nothing of the laws which relate to its adjusted parts and processes, yet we deduce enough by analogy to know that there are laws governing in the unexplored regions of creation, as certainly as in those departments which we have investigated. The order of the universe is maintained, the relations of its different parts adjusted, and the existence of the whole, and of each part in particular, preserved by law. *Law is a necessity of things;* necessary in order to process, harmony, and stability, in any system. The laws of nature, as a code, are so adjusted with each other that no one could be changed without affecting the entire system. There are links of law which bind the parts and processes of the universe from an atom to a system, from the lowest manifestation of life to the mightiest created intellect. The laws of the Creator are universal and perfect. There is no progression in a law. Other things being the same and equal, the measure and rule of law are the same forever. Man may not calculate with perfect accuracy the moment when the shadow will strike the disc of an eclipsed orb; but the error lies not in the operation of the law governing the relative bodies, but in some imperfection in the calculation, or in some related influence not taken into the account. That law is cognate with organization, and the basis of order in the universe, will be admitted by all who read these pages. Law, then, is a necessity of things—necessary to the identity and existence of the several parts of the creation, and to the harmony of the universe as a whole.

PENALTY A NECESSITY OF LAW.

Law is a necessity of things, and *penalty is a necessity of law.* This second affirmation, although equally true may not be assented to so readily as the preceding one. Sometimes there is not a clear apprehension of the difference between the necessity of penalty as a final issue, and the necessity of penalty immediately executed upon the transgressor. It is not affirmed that penalty is always immediate upon the transgression of law, nor that, where transgression has occurred, the penalty may not be counteracted. What we do say is, that every law has its penalty. Natural penalty, or rather the *penalty natural to law*, is progressive derangement tending to ultimate destruction. If disorder be not immediately destructive, then, during the deranged action which follows departure from law, the subject by interposition, as we shall see, may be recovered to obedience ; but if not recovered, the destruction of the subject, whatever it may be, *is necessary*, and therefore certain.

REASONS WHY PENALTY IS A NECESSITY OF LAW.

We wish to reiterate and illustrate this form of expression until the two cognate truths become lucid and settled convictions. We can perceive enough of the nature and relations of things to know that penalty lies not wholly, nor perhaps mostly, against the subject that transgresses the law. The necessity of penalty is connected with the general good. God has created things, as we have noticed, in relationship to each other, and the restoration or destruction of a transgressing subject is necessary to the harmony and safety of the whole.

In the realms both of matter and mind there are facts that elucidate this subject: the physical will illustrate the moral.* If a planet should "shoot madly from its sphere," its destruction would be necessary, not so much on its own account (if we may so speak), as on account of its deranging influence upon other bodies. When it lost its place and balance among the spheres, it passed into a condition of disorder which would necessarily terminate in its destruction. This, however, would not be the greatest evil. In its disorder it would necessarily encroach upon the orbits of

* "The Author of the realm of spirits is likewise the Author of the realm of nature: both kingdoms develop themselves by the same laws. Wherefore those comparisons, which the Redeemer derives from the realm of nature, are not *mere* comparisons serving to throw light upon the topic in hand; they are inward [profound] analogies, *and nature is a witness for the realm of spirits.* This truth floats dimly in the allegorizing Cabalists, and also is prevalent in Swedenborg, who did not lack in the apprehension of the principle, but only in the application of the principle. Their principle was—בעילא כל־מה די בארעא דכי נמי *i. e.*, 'every thing that is in the kingdom of the earth, is found also in the kingdom of heaven.' [*Sohar ad Gen.*, f. 91, c. 362]. Were it not so, those comparisons would not have the power of conviction which they do exercise over every unperverted mind."—Vide *Professor Tholuck of Halle on the Vine Emblem in John* xv. *rendered by Kaufman.*

other bodies, derange the whole system to which it belonged, and, if not destroyed, it would involve the whole in eventual ruin. When it left its prescribed place, then, in view of the safety of other parts of the system, its destruction would become necessary. The very laws which preserved it in its place would cause its destruction out of its place ; and in order to save it, God would have to destroy all the physical laws of the system (and then it would not be saved), or adopt some expedient to bring it back and balance the injury which its aberration had occasioned to the members of the solar family. Destruction is a necessity when any member of a system persistently violates the laws of the system.

So an animal which violates its instincts departs not only from the laws of adaptation which secure its own happiness, but, as God, has filled all departments of nature with body or life appropriate to the several conditions, when an animal leaves the sphere which the law of its instincts prescribes, it necessarily impinges upon the province of other things, and the good of the whole requires its destruction, and the nature of things secures the infliction of the penalty.

We say, *the good of the whole requires its destruction.* If the ants were to leave the earth, forget their instincts, and live upon the pollen and vital germs of the flowers, the bees would die, and fruit would cease to exist throughout the world. The ants, then, must either be destroyed, or bees and fruits, and every thing which lives upon fruits, must suffer.

We said, *the nature of things secures the infliction of the penalty.* The nature of the circumstances is such that the ant must provide food and shelter for the winter, but of the germs of flowers she could not make a winter's store; the ant, therefore, which had left its own province, as well as the bee which had not, would live a miserable life for a brief season, and then die of chill and starvation. Thus God's laws are self-executed. The nature of every thing is adapted to certain conditions; but the same laws which preserve the life of any thing in its own place, will destroy that life if it passes its prescribed limits.

ANOTHER REASON WHY PENALTY IS A NECESSTY OF LAW.

Let us look further at the last thoughts in the preceding section. Penalty is not only a necessity of law, because without order organization would cease; but it is a necessity of law in the same sense that cold is the absence of heat. Obedience to law is the condition upon which the safety and life of things depend. The constitution of each being is adapted to the conditions in which it was created to live. In its appropriate conditions there are provisions for its wants and sources of happiness for its enjoyment. So far as there is design in law, then, it indicates benevolence, which binds by law every thing in the condition where its happiness is procured and where its existence aids in producing the happiness of other things. Law and love are one in God. A beaver's instincts and conformations are adapted to the water ; but if it should stray into the desert, where the ostrich is at home, it would meet death by protracted suffering or by the violence of other animals. The bee, by obeying the laws of its life, not only secures appropriate stores for itself, but, by distributing the pollen of flowers, it aids in the germination of fruits and gives variety to the flora of the world. Thus, in obedience to the specific laws of each species, each individual not only finds happiness and life, but aids in the happiness and life of the whole. To depart from law, therefore, as necessarily secures suffering and final death, as to depart from good secures evil.

TO THE DISOBEDIENT PARDON IS IMPOSSIBLE.

To the disobedient the laws of the universe are inexorable. The law permits no transgression, and provides for no pardon. In so far as law would allow of transgression, it would annul itself and produce evil. A single transgression places the trespassers in the "road to ruin;" and pardon in itself can not, from the nature of the case, prevent or remit the penalty. Happiness and life being the result of obedience, as we have seen, pardon without a return of the transgressor to the sphere of obedience would be a form without effect. Obedience is the condition of safety and life; therefore, pardon without restoration of the transgressor to obedience is absurd and impossible in a system governed by law.

IGNORANCE DOES NOT AVERT THE PENALTY OF NATURAL LAW.

Law is inexorable in another sense than the one exhibited above. In all cases below moral law the penalty attaches to the transgressor, without reference to the manner or cause of the violation. Whether the transgressor be ignorant or enlightened—whether the act be done wilfully or of necessity—no matter in what way the subject passes from under law, it passes to penalty. Many animals are born suffering, and their life is one protracted pain until the coming on of the death-agony. In all such cases there is some structural derangement, some organic injury, which obstructs or destroys the usual operations of some function of the body.

The family who, either from ignorance or necessity, transgresses the laws of health, will suffer the penalty as certainly as though they had willingly indulged in wrong habits. If they eat injurious food, or breathe a tainted atmosphere, they will suffer, no matter in what circumstances the evil occurred. Innocent descendants, for many generations, often suffer evils induced by the transgressions of their parents. Law is more sacred than life; it must be preserved, notwithstanding many individuals, innocent of all wrong in the case, and often without an act of their own, suffer intensely, even unto death. Without the law no such individuals could exist, and the suffering of many individuals is less than the abrogation of the law, which would procure the destruction of the whole. And furthermore, the abrogation, suspension, or modification of a law, is impossible, because each law is related to all other laws, and the power which affected a single law would affect the whole constitution of things connected with it.

THE FIRST VIOLATION PRODUCES A TENDENCY TO DESTRUCTION IN WHATEVER BREAKS ESTABLISHED LAW.

When the first transgression has occurred, there is no strength or influence in the aberrating subject to restore itself. If a planet were to depart from its orbit, the first departure would give it a tendency to depart forever. As a weight upon an inclined plane, the first movement creates a momentum, which will increase until the movement is stopped by an opposing force. If one cog becomes broken in a single wheel, every revolution jars the whole machinery, and widens the fracture, until the injury is repaired or until it becomes irreparable. One departure from rectitude, under all laws, makes another more easy, and every departure increases the difficulty of a restoration to order. The very laws, as we have noticed, which hold a subject to happy obedience, operate for destruction where there has been transgression. The earth is now balanced in our system, and moves in obedience to centrifugal and centripetal forces; but if it were to move from its orbit the balance would be broken, and the disproportionate or *illegal* action of the two forces would work its destruction. This would be certain unless a sympathy latent in the whole system, or a power above the system, were to accomplish its restoration.

RESTORATION OF THE DISORDERED SUBJECT POSSIBLE WITHIN A CERTAIN LIMIT.

While it is true that the action of a subject out of obedience to law tends to increase derangement, and while there is no remedy for the derangement in the aberrating subject itself, it is likewise true that there is a reparative or recuperative energy in every system as a whole, which, if called into activity, may effect recovery. The physical conformation of an animal will, to a certain extent, and within certain limits, adapt itself to circumstances of location and climate. If one part of the body be injured, there is a *vis vitæ* in the whole, by which sound parts contribute to the recovery of parts diseased or injured.* Individuals may indulge in vices, and as a consequence injure the health of the system; but if there be a cessation of the evil habit before the constitution is injured there may be recovery; but this point being passed, entire exemption from the effects of the transgression becomes impossible. A diseased or deranged member never cures itself without compensation from other members. "When one member suffers, all suffer with it;" but if there be recuperative energy remaining in the system, there is a draft upon the whole to aid in the recovery of the part diseased. So in the physical universe, aberrations in one part are met by compensations from others, and thus the balance of the whole is preserved. These compensations seem to flow from what

* See "God in Disease, or the Manifestation of Design in Morbid Phenomena," by James D. Duncan, M.D., c. 8–10.

may be called a sympathetic principle, pervading the whole of any system, or of any distinct organization, and perhaps pervading the whole universe ; and, as has been stated, the restorative power only extends to a certain limit, beyond which the injury of the aberrating subject is irremediable. This sympathy pervading the whole is often strikingly exhibited in species of animated nature. If one animal is attacked, the cry of distress will generally arouse individuals of its proper species, and bring them to the rescue.* It is the conservative power of the whole species exerted to preserve the parts. This conservative or recuperative sympathy is an impartation of " saving health" from the Creator, pervading all systems, uniting the individuals of species, and to some extent affecting all objects of the creation.

THE RESTORATION OF THOSE INJURED BY THE TRANSGRESSOR IS ANOTHER NECESSARY CONDITION IN ORDER TO THE SAFETY AND HAPPINESS OF A SYSTEM WHERE VIOLATION OF LAW HAS OCCURRED.

When any derangement of the order established by law takes place, either in the animate or inanimate creation, it is not only necessary that the subject violating the laws appropriate to its nature should be re-

* A hybrid, in this and all other respects, is out of sympathy with all species of things.

covered, but it is necessary that the injuries which its departures from law have produced to other things should be repaired.

We refer again to a system where the effect of law on the largest scale, and in its most minute influence, can be best appreciated. If one of the solar family were to leave its path, then, in order to the safety of the system, it would not only be necessary that it should be recovered, but likewise that all evil done by its aberration should be repaired. If it were restored, while the derangement which it had caused was permitted to continue, this unrepaired derangement would increase until it had produced the destruction of the whole system. The law is not made for one, but for many; and the laws that pertain to one class are linked into those which govern another, and when one link is broken the whole system to which it pertains is deranged. So, as we have noticed, if any species of animals were to depart from its prescribed place, it would remove other species, and these again would impinge upon others, and thus derangement would go on carrying its evil influence through whole classes of animated life.

When the individuals of any species are by instinct destructive to others, there are certain armatures and instruments, aggressive and defensive, in creatures, which are wisely balanced by the Creator, for the preservation of individuals, and for destroying or preserving life, so that the whole series of species maintain a proportionate adjustment to each other. But when an *evil which violates the laws of instinct* originates in any particular creature of a species, as in the case of a rabid dog, extermination must take place, until every living thing is extirpated which was affected by the poison. Diseases produced by certain vices tend to disseminate themselves, and the recovery of one set of transgressors is of no avail unless the infection be extirpated which exists in the system of others. The transgressor must be recovered, and those affected by him restored, before the poison ceases to circulate in the blood of the race. Two things, then, are necessary in order to the removal of physical or organic derangement, in order to rectification, in all cases where there has been violation of law: first, the recovery of the transgressor to obedience; and second, the removal of the evil in others which the transgressor had occasioned.

OF MAN AS A SUBJECT OF LAW.

In the light of the preceding principles we come to consider the laws which attach to man, and to make some preliminary distinctions before noticing more particularly the moral law and its relations to man as a subject of moral government. There are at least two preliminary discriminations which it is important we should make. Many persons of good intentions, claiming to be teachers of a true and useful philosophy, have, as we think, erred themselves, and have misled others, by not making the discriminations which follow.

TWO CLASSES OF LAWS AND PENALTIES ATTACH TO MAN.

Man is a bifold being, he has a physical and a spiritual nature. There are, therefore, two classes of laws which attach themselves to him; the one to his organic, the other to his moral being. The laws which relate to man's animal organism are interwoven with our mortal constitution, and cease to affect us at the dissolution of the body. The laws which relate to our life and happiness, as moral beings, are connate with the existence of the soul, *and so long as the soul lives it must live by them and under them.* The laws which govern man—one class as a material, the other as a spiritual being—are as distinct from each other as the soul and the body. We should keep this distinction in mind, because the penalties for transgressing the organic laws, which pertain to the animal economy, are often so mingled with the penalties of moral transgression, that true views of the subject are obscured.*

PAIN IS NOT ALWAYS ULTIMATE PENALTY.

If pain be considered penalty, which it may be in one sense, yet pain is not all the penalty of transgressing either organic or moral law. It is part of the penalty only, as progress is part of the result—as derangement is linked with disaster. Pain indicates that there is disease or derangement in the system. If the disorder be removed by compensation from other parts of the system, or by appliances from without, the pain ceases with the removal of the derangement by which it was occasioned. The pain was neither the disease nor the cure. A cancer is a different thing from the pain which it produces. Often the pain abates although there be no remedy for the evil. "*Dying, thou shalt die,*" is the penalty of transgressing the laws both of our organic and moral nature. That is, derangement, when begun, tends to and will ultimate in death. Such, too, as we shall see, is the penalty of the moral law. The nature and design of all laws are the same. The necessity of penalty and the nature of penalty are the same in all cases. The best expression for penalty

* As in the works of Fowler, which contain some practical truth, with many erroneous views and conceited assumptions.

which can be formed is that found in the earliest Hebrew Scriptures, and attached to the first disobedience —"Dying, thou shalt die." *

Let us, then, not mistake pain of body or pain of conscience for the derangement itself, which causes the pain, or for the final penalties of organic or moral law. Pain often abates in the body as the strength of the constitution diminishes to death. Pain may subserve a benevolent design; it is admonitory of existing disorder, or of penalty in progress. But the fact is beyond dispute that *death* ensues as the *ultimate penalty*, whether with or without pain, unless the disorder be removed.

* Gen. ii. 17, "Thou shalt surely die." [Heb. *Dying, thou shalt die.*] From the period of transgression a dying life is ordained; a moral derangement, which, without rescue, will ensue in a hopeless death.

CHAPTER II.

CONCERNING THE MORAL LAW

IT has been stated that the nature and necessity of law and penalty are the same in all cases. *God is one,* and all law exists eternally in and by the Uncreated Mind. We shall now consider the Moral Law alone, and notice that the principles of the foregoing exposition are as applicable to the Moral Law as to any other law by which God governs his universe.

NECESSITY, INVIOLABILITY, AND SANCTION OF MORAL LAW.

If God be a moral being and a moral governor, there must be a moral law. We can not suppose a moral governor without a moral law; in reason, the one implies the other.

As the Supreme Being is the moral governor of the universe, the moral law can be nothing else than an expression of his will; if, therefore, the character of the Divine Being be perfectly holy and immutable, the moral law must be so.

Like other laws, the moral law is inexorable—it can not license or pardon transgression. To suppose that the law could permit sin, would be to say either that God is unholy, or that he permitted what is contrary to his own will, which is absurd.

Besides, if God is benevolent, he would not license sin, because, as we have seen, the transgression involves evil to the transgressor. God would not, therefore, as a benevolent being, permit sin, except as a part of a system where progress and compensations were introduced, that would in the end remove the evil or bring good out of it.

The characteristic of inviolability in the law is adjusted to the moral convictions of the beings who are subject to it. No one can, without doing violence to his reason and conscience, affirm that God ought to make a law that would license a single sin. The holy inviolability of the law finds a sanction in the moral constitution of every intelligent subject of God's government. No sane man will say, even in his own case, that God ought to make a law that would permit him to commit a single transgression.

Now, if God can not, from the necessities of his nature, make a law that will permit sin; if he *ought not* to make such a law, and if he has so constituted man that, as a moral being, he can not approve of such a law—then, the force of all these considerations combined, puts the truth beyond question, that the moral law of God, like all other laws, can not permit a single transgression. And, while it allows of no sin, it makes no provision for pardon. The promise of life is on the one only condition of perfect and perpetual obedience. No law can proclaim pardon for the transgression of its own requirements without annulling itself. It may provide, in some cases, for compensation—as for an injury inflicted a compensation may be rendered to the person injured ; but to provide a pardon for the transgression of its own precept is not in the nature of law.

Besides, as in other laws, if pardon were offered to a sinner without obedience, the proposition would be preposterous, and the promise a nullity, because God has constituted the soul, as he has all things else, that life is found only in obedience. To pardon a sinner, therefore, while he continues a sinner, is morally impossible, and were it possible, in any sense, under the Divine government, it would be without benefit to man.

MORAL TRANSGRESSION TENDS TO PENAL DESTRUCTION.

As in other instances, the first departure from obedience in man creates a tendency to continued departing. Any derangement, either in the physical or moral system is self-aggravating and self-perpetuating, without aid from other parts. A single act of sin is a departure from rectitude, and the departure strengthens the depraved tendency. Sin enfeebles man's moral nature. The conservative or recuperative power of his moral constitution grows less by every act of transgression. Conscience becomes less potential, and the will more inclined to err; in other words, the strength of moral emotion is abated, and evil inclination strengthened by every act of transgression. As the exercise of any bodily member increases its strength, so the exercise of our moral faculties, whether in a good or bad direction, increases the inclination of the will to good or evil. Thus sin begets sin. The power of sin over the soul increases by sinning. This is human experience, and it agrees with human observation in relation to the effect of transgression in all other cases. One sin puts the soul in the "road to ruin" as certainly as the first movement of a weight down an inclined plane tends to accelerate momentum and to prevent return.

NECESSITY OF THE DEATH-PENALTY IN MORAL LAW.

The death-penalty exists in moral law by the same necessity that it does in physical and organic laws. It may not be in view of the evil, as it affects the transgressor only that the penalty is pronounced : "the soul that sinneth, it shall die." It may be, certainly is, in view likewise of the evil, as it affects the good of others, that the irreclaimable transgressor is doomed to moral death.

The moral law is universal in its application to moral beings. It binds all angels and all men to love God supremely, and their neighbor as themselves. Sin not only injures the moral character of the transgressor, but evil influence and evil example produce evil in other subjects of the same moral government. If sin had no evil effect upon beings of a sphere higher than that of man, still it has the twofold effect of injuring the transgressor and of imparting injury to others of his own class in the moral world. But analogy teaches that all beings bound by the same laws are, or may be, affected by each other's transgressions ; and likewise, that classes related in the same economy affect each other as individuals ; and this relationship must continue so long as law exists, and so long as spirits continue free, whether in this world or the next. The death-penalty, then, in moral law, is necessary, for the same reasons that exist in all other cases. Unless there can be restoration to obedience, and compensation for the evil done, the good of the whole demands the destruction of the transgressor.

ADDITIONAL REASON FOR THE DEATH-PENALTY IN MORAL LAW.

In addition to the reasons which have been mentioned, reasons connected with law in all departments of the universe, that the death-penalty is necessary in order to the good of the whole system, there are *moral considerations*, which add their weight in cases where the *moral law* is transgressed. Every one can see that an agent, knowing good and evil, is not only bound by moral obligations to benefit others, but when he does a moral act which he knows will produce injury to other beings, he is guilty for that moral injury as well as for the injury done to himself. In all unreasoning things there can be only a legal connection between transgression and its consequences. But human transgression has this necessary *legal* connection with its consequences; and besides this, a knowledge of the wrong adds moral guilt to transgression. The evil done to others, likewise, of which he has knowledge, is often numerically and morally greater than that which accrues to himself, as the interests of many are greater than the interests of one. In moral law, therefore, pardon and compensation to avert the consequences of evil done to others is especially necessary. The restoration must go further than the recovery of the individual transgressor, because the evil goes further. A sinner who has influenced others to evil is guilty, in part at least, for the evil in others as well as for that in himself. His own restoration, or return to obedience, covers only a portion of the evil growing out of his transgression. The currents of rebellion which the sinner, before repentance, originated or accelerated in other minds, do not cease with his death or repentance; they run on in the life-stream of others. A transgressor may be—he often is—restored to obedience himself, while those whom he influenced to sin continue in the ways of disobedience. As one may recover from a contagious disease while those die to whom he communicated his disorder, so one may repent from disobedience while those whom he influenced previously to his penitence continue disobedient subjects of the Divine government; and unless there be recuperative moral energy in the system to which the sinner, with his deranged moral nature, belongs, there can be no restoration of the offender, and therefore no pardon;

and even if he be restored, the guilt which he caused in others continues, and restoration or compensation in their case is needed before the effects of his sin are removed or counteracted, and before he can be pardoned according to law.

The death-penalty, then, accrues under the moral as it does under organic and physical laws, but with additional moral considerations enforcing its necessity. From this death-penalty of moral law, for moral transgression, there can be no redemption, except by restoration of the transgressor to obedience, and compensation for the evil which his sin has occasioned in the moral government of God.

RECAPITULATION.*

Of the things which we have written this is the sum. Law and penalty are not chimeras, nor incidental and mutable relations of things; they are necessities of the creation. Law is higher and holier than life; it is necessary to the existence of life. Penalty is a necessity of law; it is necessary to the existence of law: it is necessary to the good of the whole. Where transgression exists, pardon, or happiness, or safety is impossi-

* We recapitulate frequently in this portion of the work, in order that the reader may observe the connection of each chapter with conclusions ascertained in preceding ones.

ble. Law is inexorable. Ignorance of its provisions does not avert the penalty of either physical or organic laws, and only qualifies or graduates the penalty of moral law. The first transgression puts penalty in progress, and places the subject in the road to ruin. Restoration to order and obedience is possible within certain limits ; but safety is impossible and pardon absurd, unless two conditions are complied with, viz. :— *the restoration of the transgressor, and the restoration of those affected by his influence ;* or, *restoration of the transgressor, and compensation which will counterwork and eventually remove the derangement from the system.* In cases of derangement, recovery or compensation can not be accomplished by the deranged subject, but must arise from sources out of or above the derangement ; but one or the other, restoration or destruction, is necessary and certain.

In the application of these general principles to man, there are two classes of laws which apply—one to his organism as a corporeal being, the other to his spiritual nature. The penalties of organic sins are inflicted upon the body, and are, therefore, temporal and legal : spiritual penalties are inflicted upon the soul. Unless there be restoration, penalty continues while the life of the subject lasts. Pain that accompanies derangement is not the whole of penalty ; it indicates that derangement exists, and accompanies it until restoration or destruction ensue. When recovery is not effected, the destruction of the subject is the natural and necessary penalty of transgression.

The moral law, in its application to man as a spiritual being, possesses the same characteristics as physical and organic laws. Its nature is inviolable and inexorable, and its penalties immutable. There may be pardon after obedience is restored, and compensation for evils made, which the transgressor himself can not effect; but without these, "dying, thou shalt die," is decreed by legal, natural, and moral necessity; die spiritually, by the subject's own sin, and in order to secure the system from the effect of disordered action.

CHAPTER III.

MAN UNABLE TO RECOVER HIMSELF FROM DISOBEDIENCE OR REDEEM HIMSELF FROM THE PENALTIES OF SIN.

In the light of preceding principles, the *legal* conditions of rectification, or justification, in the sight of the law, are plain. They are twofold: first, a restoration of the transgressor to obedience to law; and, second, a reparation of all injuries occasioned to himself and to others by past disobedience. If the transgressor could recover himself to perfect obedience—if he could repair the evil done to his own moral nature by sin—if he could counteract the evil effect of his past life in other minds, and compensate for the evil which those minds did in consequence of his influence upon them; then, being rectified himself by his own power, and having rectified the injury which he had occasioned, if God is sufficiently merciful to forgive sin, the sinner would be admitted again into place and favor in the Divine government. And still, under these circumstances, if they were possible, the pardon of the moral transgressor would be an act of mercy, because an evil act is wrong in itself, and subsequent obedience and reparation, while they prevent further evil consequences, do not atone for the evil *per se* of the wrong action. But God is merciful; the transgressor, therefore, if he could perform these necessary conditions, would be pardoned.

But to fulfill these conditions necessary to justification and pardon is as much beyond the power of a sinful being as to create a world. With no aid from without himself, man, as a sinner, must fall under the death-penalty induced by the violation of law. So far as ability to recover himself is concerned, and so far as present penalty is connected with present sin, he is already dead.

GROUNDS OF MAN'S MORAL INABILITY TO SAVE HIMSELF.

The statements in a preceding section, showing the nature of sin to aggravate itself, are mainly applicable here. The commission of sin does not abate the disposition to transgress, but increases it. Like all other derangements, the tendency to sin augments itself by its own action. Transgression enfeebles the moral nature. Conscience becomes less potential, and the inclination of the will to evil increases with every act of transgression. Habit produces facility in any direction to which the will may tend; and all things, as we have seen, are so constituted that any aberration from the line of law decreases the power which holds subjects of law in their place, and gives strength to the influence which draws them from obedience. As a stream passing over a rock wears for itself a channel from which it can not escape, so the will, moving in obedience to a selfish inclination, is alienated from the standard of rectitude, and confirms itself, by its natural action, in opposition to the Divine Law. Affectionate obedience to God, and affectionate effort for human good, is holiness; but the transgressor has not only lost his holiness, but his disposition to be holy. As inclination is to a falling body, so disposition is to the mind. Restoration, therefore, without light and aid from without the soul itself, is morally impossible. On the other hand, the natural tendency is to depart, not to return.

MAN CAN NOT COMPENSATE FOR THE INJURY WHICH HIS SINS HAVE OCCASIONED IN OTHER MINDS.

If man were able to renovate his own moral nature and restore himself to obedience, his return would not make amends for past injuries done to others. A good act in the present does not compensate for a bad one in the past. It is unreasonable to suppose that a man can atone for killing one person by subsequently saving the life of another, because good within the compass of our knowledge and ability is an ever-present duty; and the performance of duty can purchase no pardon for the past nor indulgence for the future.

And if our return to obedience, by whatsoever power it may be effected, can not atone for past sin in ourselves, much less can our obedience arrest, or atone for, the evil which our sin occasioned, and which continues to flow on in other minds. No man sins without injuring others, either by neglect of duty or by wrong example. The wrong bias left upon other minds continues, and these minds again influence others to evil. Thus every man who has injured others by an example of disobedience, leaves an evil influence in the world after his own individual evil action has ceased by repentance or by death.

The facts and the philosophy included in these considerations make it plain to us that man being a transgressor of the moral law, and liable to the death-penalty, can not restore himself to obedience, nor purchase pardon by compensating for the past evils of his life; hence, if man is ever restored to obedience, and pardoned for past sin, it must be by the aid of a Power without and above himself.

CHAPTER IV.

THE LEGAL ASPECT AND PRACTICAL VALUE OF THE SACRIFICE OF CHRIST, AND ITS ACCORDANCE WITH THE LAW OF PROGRESS AND THE CHARACTER OF GOD.

WE have shown clearly, as we think, that in order to the pardon of a transgressor, who is liable as a subject of moral government, it is not only necessary that he should be recovered from transgression himself, but it is necessary that he should be able to repair the injury which his sin has occasioned in the moral system of which he forms a part. This responsibility grows out of the fact that he is an integral part of a moral system that is a whole in itself. We have shown further, that no man has ability to restore himself to obedience, or to rectify the evil which he has caused to other moral beings by his sin. Light, love, and influence are conditions of repentance, and these must come, as we have seen, from without and above the transgressor. We inquire now concerning the legal aspect of the sacrifice of Christ, as governmental compensation for sin, and a legal condition of the pardon and justification of the sinner.

We assume again, that perfect obedience to the moral law is the legal or constitutional ground of justification; that is, it is the thing which the nature of the system, and of the subject, requires. Every man's sin has, as a matter of fact, injured himself and others. He has thus rendered himself liable to the penalty of the law, and, within himself, he has no power to restore his own soul, or to compensate for his evil influence. In looking for *legal* justification, then, we must inquire if there be any being belonging to the same system, and amenable to the same government with ourselves, whose merit rises above the demands of the law. If such a being could be found, then his super-legal merit, compensating for human demerit, might balance the moral system, and bring the sum of the superior and inferior agencies into accordance with the claims of the legal principle. (This compensation of whole parts suffering loss, in order to restore injured members, is, as we have shown, a law in the nature of things.) But in order that these agencies should balance each other, they must *practically counter-work each other;* that is, the evil consequences of human sin must be counteracted, or *worked out of the system,* by the merit of transcendent holiness, *because rectification of the evil is necessary to justification in law.* If such a meritorious and efficient agent as this could be found, then the penitent transgressor might, by this merit, be restored, and the consequences of his sin counteracted or removed.

Now the moral law could not demand the sacrifice of Christ, His perfect obedience fulfilled all its requirements. Sacrifice can not be required of a guiltless being to save the guilty from penalty. Law does not demand it, but LOVE, as the *recuperative* power of the system, prompts it. Such a self-sacrifice for others is super-legal, and if this mercy and merit above law can be brought into efficient relation to those below law, the two agencies may not only balance each other, *but they will balance each other*, as a superior moral agency will counter-work a weaker one, *if the one be efficiently united with the other.* Thus, the merit of Christ above law becomes, by faith (as we shall see), an efficient moral power which restores the transgressor to obedience, and compensates, as a recuperative energy in the moral system of which man is a part.

This is the algebra* of redemption—the abstract ex-

* The foundation principles of the physical universe in its matter and motions are mathematical, and it is certain that the *moral* relations of things are alike permanent and proportionate in their nature. Let no one, then, suppose that such deductions as this are altogether empty and irrelevant.

pression which lies back of the personal and practical application of the subject. Or, rather, it is the actual value of Christ's merit, applied to the governmental requirements which relate to the pardon of sin.

If law were absolute in itself—if there were no supreme Law-giver above the law, who could maintain its sanctions while he interposed to avert the penal consequences of transgression, it would not be possible, in the nature of things, to save any transgressor from the penalties of sin. If any transgressor be saved, therefore, it must be by an interposition of the Law-giver who maintains the law, while mercy restores the offender. *Power above law is not justice nor mercy, but merit above law is both.* Divine interposition, therefore, to save the lost, would be a substitute of its own merit to maintain the law, while mercy interposed to redeem the sinner. Thus "God might be just and the Justifier of every one that believeth."

If such equations and compensations in law pervade the physical universe, why not moral compensation in the moral universe?

Says the famous Anselm, archbishop of Canterbury in the eleventh century, in his treatise *Cur Deus homo*—a treatise which the mathematicians Leibnitz and Hegel have spoken of in the highest terms—speaking of the incarnation of the son of God, Anselm says in substance, as rendered by J. F. Clarke:—"To make satisfaction, this God-man must pay something that he does not owe on his own account. As a man, he owes perfect obedience for himself; this, then, can not be the satisfaction; but being a sinless man, he is not bound to die; his death, therefore, as the death of the God-man, is the adequate and proper satisfaction."

Here, then, the question of personal interest presents itself: *Has the Creator interposed in the moral world, by adjustment and new creation,* to remove the consequences of sin, and to elevate men into His own moral image? We inquire for the fact:

DOES THE SACRIFICE OF CHRIST ACTUALLY COUNTERWORK THE EVILS OF SIN?

That faith in the sacrifice of Christ, as an exhibition of the love of God for man, does counteract sinful propensities and habits in believers, can not be doubted. The reasons and relations of this great truth are clear, and have been already suggested. Jesus assumed, as the object of faith, that character, and manifested those qualities, which he desires shall be produced in believers. *He personified love and obedience. His life-history and love-death were the living and dying impersonation of these graces. He assumed objectively what man needs to be subjectively;* and as by faith the attributes of the object of love become subjective in the believer, hence the life and sacrifice of Christ, appropriated by faith, must, from the nature of things, transform believers into the Saviour's image, becausc they will receive "grace for grace." Thus by the efficacy of faith, in accordance with the laws of mind, Christ is formed in the soul "the hope of glory." Beholding the light of the glory of God in the face of Christ, believers are transformed "into the same image, from glory to glory, even as by the Spirit of the Lord."

The view we are considering may be exhibited in a logical form as follows:—The history of the Church and personal Christian experience confirm the fact beyond question, that those who truly believe will be influenced in their conscience, will, and affections, by the character of Christ. But Christ is the objective type of love and obedience to God; hence those who believe in Christ, so far as the objective model becomes subjective by faith, are restored to love and obedience to God.

Thus it is that faith in Christ subdues the spirit of rebellion, and works by love and purifies the heart. An efficient relation is established, by which the soul is drawn back to the sphere of love and obedience from which it had departed. The merit of the process is in the objective model, because the subjective effect is produced by the objective efficacy; hence as justification in the sight of the law is, by the merit of Christ, so sanctification is by faith in that merit. The conclusion results, therefore, clear as light, and weighty as gold—that by the moral merit of Christ alone believers are legally justified in the sight of God.

THE MERIT OF CHRIST COUNTERACTS, AND COMPENSATES FOR, THE EFFECT OF SIN UPON OTHERS.

We come now to the second thing legally or systematically * necessary in order to redemption from the penalty of transgression. Does the merit of Christ avail to counteract the consequences of sin, as those consequences affect others beside the transgressor? The sinner, as we have noticed, by his example and influence produces evil in other minds: his own restoration by repentance and faith does not remove the evil of which he was the cause. Now, does the work of Christ tend to counterwork not only the evils of sin as they affect the transgressor, but as they likewise affect other moral agents?

Christ's love-sacrifice is a source of actual saving power, which brings those who truly believe back to affectionate obedience to God. Thus far, then, the relations between God and man are adjusted; but, as we have shown, the individual transgressor may be restored, while those who were affected by his sin before his restoration still go on in transgression; and the restored transgressor has no power to arrest the pro-

* The acceptation in which I use this word in this place is a needful one, and one which I will venture to propose, especially in philosophical inquiries. *Systematical*—that which is necessary as a part of a system—necessary in view of the nature of a system as a whole.

gress of the evil, and no merit to compensate for the injury which he has occasioned, and which still operates in the minds of others. But as the moral government of God *is one*—bound together by one law, "Thou shalt love the Lord thy God with all thy heart, and thy neighbor as thyself"—the rectification of evil consequences in the system is necessary, in order to legal justification. Does, then, Christ's sacrifice compensate for—remove the effects of, my sin from the minds of others; and the effects of evil induced by the influence of others from my mind?

In the case of each individual that is restored to obedience, his own sinful habits, whether produced by his own depraved propensities or by the influence of others, are broken, and a countervailing influence is established, which will in the end eradicate the evil from the heart. The effect of a man's sin in other minds does not flow backward, but forward. The stream of evil that one man originates in the minds of others, runs forward in the life-history of individuals toward the end of time. Suppose an individual pursuing his own inclinations, and affected at the same time by my bad example; he is arrested in his life of disobedience, and now truly believes in Christ. The character and love of Jesus becoming operative by faith changes his will—a will wrongly determined by natural inclination and strengthened in that determination by my example. So the power of Christ's merit meets the aggregate of evil in penitents, whether that evil be produced by their own evil inclinations, or by the influence of others. It reaches the sources of demerit, and substitutes a countervailing power in the heart. If, then, in the progress of human history, those evil effects which I or others have occasioned, should be met as they flow on in the minds of men, and when met, be counteracted by the efficacy of the love-sacrifice, then I, having been before restored, and the effects of my sin being now counteracted, my evil would be removed from the system of which I form a part, and the law of the system would have nothing against me.

Now history declares, and the Bible frequently and explicitly affirms the great truth, that the fountain of love opened at Calvary sends forth a stream that augments in volume and in power—checked at times, but then again bursting the barrier, and flowing onward in the course of time. The flowing blood of Jesus, purifying from sin, is the rich and affecting symbol of this divine efficacy, which is finally to "fill the earth," to "take away the sins of the world." The time, therefore, will actually come, when all the effects of my sin upon myself, and all the effects of my sin in others, which remain in the current of the world's moral history, will be met and counteracted by the power of love exhibited in the sacrifice of Christ. The first Adam, as a living being, originated a stream of evil which descended in the life-flow of the race ; the second Adam, as a life-giving Spirit, originated a stream of mercy, which meets the dark current and sweetens it into love. Thus the flow of the Love-Fountain* will in the end purify the earth from sin and uncleanness."

COMPENSATION BY THE SACRIFICE OF CHRIST AS IT OPERATES THROUGH HUMAN AGENCY.

In addition to this compensatory merit of Christ, viewed in its entireness, the sacrifice of Christ causes a reaction against sin, which is compensation in an instrumental form for the evil influence which the redeemed sinner has exerted upon other minds. When the believer is restored to obedience, he exercises thenceforward a healthful influence over other minds, inclining them to penitence and faith. The first effect of the love of Christ upon human souls moves them to influence others to love and obedience. So the merit of Christ not only restores the alienated mind, but it secures, through that mind, a salutary influence upon other moral agents. *The redeemed soul is not only restored, but it is imbued with an influence which is restorative.*

* "In those days I will open a fountain."

An accumulative process thus goes on ; every restored mind adding to the power of the reaction originated by Christ against sin. As individuals are restored in Christ, the *recuperative energy of the race is increased.* Thus, in accordance with the laws of the system, and of individual agency, is the Saviour of sinners taking away the sins of the world.

The conclusion then is reached, that there is efficacy in the sacrifice of Christ to restore the believer to affectionate obedience, and to counteract the effect of his sin in the lives of other moral agents. Christ's love-sacrifice was *remedial and compensatory*, "offered by the Eternal Spirit, once for all, for the sins of the world." Amen.

Having noticed that the sacrifice of Christ adjusts the claims of moral government, and by faith practically counterworks the evil of sin, we are prepared in succeeding chapters to consider other vital relations of Christ's manifestation, as they connect themselves with the redemption of man.

CHAPTER V.

THE MEANS, MEASURES, AND METHODS OF RESTORATION TO OBEDIENCE TO THE DIVINE LAW-GIVER.

ASSUMING now, that by the *compensating* and *efficient* righteousness of Christ man can be saved from spiritual disorder and death, the inquiry presents itself—How could aid be granted in adaptation to the nature and wants of man as a voluntary responsible being? The meritorious sacrifice being offered for his redemption in the counsel of God,* what are the necessary means and methods by which the power of atoning mercy may become efficient upon the soul of man as an intelligent and responsible being?

KNOWLEDGE OF THE DIVINE CHARACTER COMMUNICATED BY THE ONLY METHOD ADAPTED TO ENLIGHTEN THE MIND, WHILE AT THE SAME TIME IT AWAKENED THE SUSCEPTIBILITIES OF MAN.

It is a truth not only plainly revealed in the Scriptures, but affirmed in the reason of our race, that man's best condition is attained by assimilation to the

* "Slain before the foundation of the world."

character of God. But in order that we should become conformed to the Divine character, that character must be clearly and impressively revealed to us. The Divine Mind must be known to us, not only as a being of power and wisdom, but as a Godhead of conscience, affections, and will. The human can not be transformed into another species. The perfection of our proper powers is the final end of our nature. To quicken the conscience, purify the susceptibilities, and guide the will, and thus fully develop the moral powers of our species, is to advance man to his ultimate attainment. For this end the distinctive revelation of the moral attributes of God is necessary, in order that each human faculty may assume the lineaments of the Divine.

THE DIVINE BEING HAS AN IMMUTABLE CHARACTER.

No one doubts but that the Supreme Being (blessed be His name!) has a defined and settled moral character; but men have widely different, and often contradictory views of what that character is. One man believes God possesses certain moral attributes, and another believes he does not; to suppose that both are right would be absurd, because a thing can not be and be at the same time.

Assuming, then, what will not be questioned, that God possesses a distinctive and permanent moral character, it follows that every man who has not a true conception of that character must be in darkness to some extent; many having very imperfect and inadequate views of God, while the conceptions of others are utterly false, and sometimes directly opposite to the truth.

THE IDEA WHICH MEN ENTERTAIN OF GOD IS A SOURCE OF EFFICIENT INFLUENCE IN FORMING THEIR CHARACTERS.

The *idea* of God, or the conception of the divine character by the mind, is all with which man, in his present condition, can be conversant. The existence and attributes of the Divine Being can have no influence upon human minds only so far as the Divine character is apprehended, and in proportion to the strength of faith which realizes God's being and presence as Maker, Saviour, and Judge of men. Knowledge gives form to the impression, and faith gives measure to its power.* If, therefore, the idea of God in the mind be one thing, and the real character of the Divine Being a different thing, the wrong idea not only

* Knowledge is the *property* and faith the *force* which brings God and man within related distance of each other.

excludes the salutary influence of right impressions, but it produces an effect upon human character injurious in proportion to the fallacy and strength of the conception. So far forth as men have false views of God before their minds when they worship, they worship a false God, and receive, as a consequence, false and injurious impressions. It is clear, therefore, that there can be no process of redemption from ignorance and sin until man receives a revelation of the true attributes of God.

THE MORAL ATTRIBUTES OF GOD CAN NOT BE REVEALED PERFECTLY, BY THE CREATION IN ITS PRESENT CONDITION.

From the design and adaptation seen in the things that are made, men infer the existence of the Supreme Being, and the infinite power and wisdom of the Godhead; but the circumscribed views which they must necessarily take of the creation as a whole, disclose to them very imperfectly the moral attributes of the Creator. If some being could stand in the present, and extend his vision over all the geological series of the past, and then forward until the cycle of the earth's progress terminates in perfection, then predicating his induction upon a perfect creation, he might, as we have shown in our first book, learn more of the moral attributes of the Divine mind. But in the present condition of things, the limitation of human vision, and the evils, or rather imperfections, noticeable in the creation, preclude the possibility of learning, from the things that are made, all that man needs to know of the moral character of the Maker.

THE ORDER OF NATURE MAY REVEAL THE NATURAL, BUT NOT THE MORAL GOODNESS OF GOD.

When, in connection with the design apparent in the adaptation of things, we study the arrangements visible in what is often called *the general providence* of God, the *natural care* (allow the expression) of the Creator for his creatures, is apparent. The succession of the seasons, the alternation of seed-time and harvest, the provision made in nature for the supply of all animal wants, indicate the care and kindness of the Creator in sustaining and preserving the creatures which he has made. But the general providence of God regards all creatures alike, irrespective of moral character or desert. The order of nature is related only to the temporal condition of living beings. From the observation of providence men may infer with certain philosophers, that God cares for classes, not for individuals ; or with certain Jews, that the measure of Divine favor to individuals is the amount of temporal good conferred upon any one. But so long as many sentient beings, capable of suffering, and yet incapable of sin, are born in pain, and live in pain till they die, the moral attributes of God, viewed in the light of providence, will be seen obscurely by the human reason. So long as virtue often suffers until death from the slanderer's malice, the rich man's avarice, or the unjust man's oppressions—so long as the innocent suffer in consequence of the crimes of others, in which they had no agency, and for which suffering they have no redress—so long as temporal providences do not redress moral wrongs—no interpretation of the ways or works of God, as exhibited in the present creation, can give to men true knowledge of the moral character of the Maker. The *natural goodness* of God, in providing for the things which he has made, may be inferred in a general sense, from the order of nature and the fitness of things; but from creation in a state of progress, before it has reached the perfect, God must be imperfectly known.

THE MORAL CHARACTER OF GOD CAN BE REVEALED ONLY THROUGH A BEING THAT POSSESSES A MORAL NATURE.

No being can manifest an attribute of its Maker unless that attribute is impressed upon its nature, or may be inferred from the relations which God has constituted between it and other things. The Creator could not reveal justice, or conscience, or holiness, through beings which possess no such attributes. There is nothing in inferior animals, or in inanimate things, that can communicate or illustrate the nature of moral attributes. These must be learned from moral beings, and from the administration of moral government. Moral qualities can be manifested only through a being that possesses those qualities; and as man alone, of all things created in our world, is endowed with these, hence he is the only being through whom and to whom may be manifested the moral attributes of the Creator.

This conclusion may be strengthened by the reason of the case. Would not human nature be a better medium through which the Divine Logos might reveal himself than any inferior nature? Would it be unworthy of God, or discordant with reason, that the Divine attributes should be fully and truly revealed through the highest nature and the only moral nature upon the earth? As God has made man capable of knowing his true character, and placed him, as a moral being in an imperfect world, where he can not know it without revelation, is it not due to man that such a revelation shall be made? Would God permit himself to be imperfectly manifested to beings capable of comprehending his true character, while yet he withheld a true manifestation of himself by a nature capable of revealing what men need to know in order to their highest good? The simple statement of the case is adapted to induce the conviction that as a human being is the only medium adapted to the highest manifestation of the Godhead, hence humanity would be the medium or mediator through which final or perfect knowledge of God would be revealed to men.

AN ADMISSION AND AN OBJECTION CONSIDERED.

At this point those who reject the doctrine of the *special revelation* of God in Christ will admit our conclusion. It is admitted, say they, that human nature is the best and only adequate medium of Divine communication, but God has bestowed moral faculties upon all human beings, therefore, every human being manifests the moral character of God, because it is a necessary inference that he who bestows moral faculties upon any class of creatures, must himself possess a moral nature. God may bestow inferior faculties, but he can not bestow faculties superior to his own.

We admit the inference that he who bestows moral faculties must have a moral nature. Let it be agreed that every sane man, in whose life the action of moral faculties is apparent, manifests, in some degree, the moral character of God. But while all thoughtful minds harmonize in this conclusion, another question arises out of this aspect of the subject. While it is granted that humanity in its present state indicates that God is a moral being, yet man, in his present condition, is an *imperfect moral being.* He has an imperfect moral nature, adapted to the present imperfect condition of the earth.* Can, then, the perfect moral excellence of God be derived from the natural character of man as a being, or from humanity as a genus?

A PERFECT HUMANITY NECESSARY TO THE PERFECT MANIFESTATION OF GOD.

Whoever may doubt about the Christian doctrine of original sin, or of actual sin existing from the commencement of moral agency, all will agree that from some cause, known or unknown to us, there is no human being that possesses a perfect mind in a perfect body—a perfect moral and corporeal nature. Every mirror of humanity, from which God's moral attributes are reflected upon the reason of men, is obscured by imperfections, so as to distort, in some degree at least,

* Eden symbolizes the perfect man in a perfect condition. The imperfect man and the thorns and thistles agree. Man is now a *cultivating* and a *cultivable* animal. Man cultivates the earth. God cultivates man. Earth-culture elevates man in a physical and social condition. Soul-culture elevates him as a spiritual and immortal being.

the Divine image. "The brightness of the Father's glory, and the precise image of his person," can be reflected with perfect accuracy from no merely human mind ever created. God can not manifest his attributes in a perfect manner through an imperfect medium. No human being ever possessed perfection in conscience, affections, and will; hence no being of our race could reveal truly the Divine attributes, *even in kind.* This being true, the creation of a perfect and special humanity was necessary, in order to accomplish the manifestation of the Divine in the human. The moral attributes of God could be revealed in kind only through a *perfect man*, and as no such man existed, or could exist, in the human family, hence the creation of a perfect humanity, or a second Adam was necessary in order to communicate to man a true knowledge of God.*

AN ALLEGED DIFFICULTY CONSIDERED.

At this point again a difficulty is interposed, which needs to be considered. It is said God can reveal truth

* Under the Old Testament dispensation, the idea of the perfect was actualized by their rites of purification and ceremonial sanctification. (See *Phil. of Plan of Salvation*, chap. vii.) Under the New Testament dispensation, the idea is realized in the humanity of Jesus, the second Adam; so that the perfect—a conception required in order to the culture of man's moral nature—is given in both dispensations.

in precept by an imperfect humanity ; we might, therefore, by inspiration, instruct men in the knowledge of his moral nature. An American writer—to whose work we have occasion frequently to refer in this part of our subject—has discussed this vital inquiry,* and has, we think, clearly shown that perfect precept is not all that is necessary to convey a knowledge of the Divine character to the human mind. Man needs a revelation to his heart as well as to his intellect. *Light* is not *love,* nor *life,* nor *power,* in a moral sense. Divine love can not be revealed by precept alone. Affinities and sympathies enter into the nature of love, and its power is rendered effective by self-denial. Love *feels* and *acts;* and a revealment of love must be a history of love-action, not a definition of what love is. Hence a fleshly manifestor, a living being, acting by the promptings of infinite love, could alone reveal the divine to the human.

Living love is *generative*—love begets love—every living thing begets its kind. Hence the didactic utterance, even if the definition were perfect, could not communicate the Divine love to the human soul. A living being † was therefore necessary, in order to manifest

* Phil. of Plan of Salvation.

† "If this view of the case be a right one, the revelation which reason demands can not be one merely of moral principles or axioms. *It must be a revelation of a living being.* It can not, therefore, be one in

the living love of God. Hence God interposed visibly and temporally in the Old Testament, and visibly and personally in the New, in order to beget love for the Lawgiver in the human heart. "The law came by Moses, grace and truth by Jesus Christ."

A FINAL DIFFICULTY CONSIDERED.

It may be said that if God were to create a second perfect man—a special humanity—with body and soul free from imperfections, and if the faculties of this perfect man were moved by Divine influence up to the amount of their capacity, this would be no more than the production of a perfect man, a humanity perfectly developed. It is true that, unless superhuman manifestations were made through the perfect human, we should only learn the true nature of man. If no manifestation were made through the perfect man above the measure of human capability, we could perceive no more of God than might be inferred from the maker of the perfect human. But the moral powers of the human would be *perfect in kind*, and then, if the

which events are merely accidents, that can be separated from some idea which has tried to embody itself in them. Facts may be only the drapery of doctrines; but they would seem to be the only possible method of manifestation for the Being—the Essential Reason."—*Maurice's Kingdom of Christ.*

infinite were revealed in these—if, in connection with the perfect human, there was revealed an indwelling divinity, which, when occasion required, developed attributes perfect in kind up to *infinity* in strength, then that mysterious union of the *Infinite* with the *perfect finite* would reveal *Divinity* and *perfect humanity* conjoined in the person of an Immanuel—GOD WITH US.

THE RESULT.

The result of these views combined is, that in order to a true manifestation of the character of God to man, a perfect humanity was necessary—a mediator between God and man. This being given, the moral image of God in man would be freed from imperfection. *The image of the Maker in kind, but not in degree**—finite, but not infinite, would be revealed in the world.

Having now the finite image of God in the perfect human, in order to manifest the Divine nature, the infinite must be seen to dwell in and act through the finite. Almighty power and wisdom, conjoined with the perfect finite, would unite the divine and human in the one person of Christ. The two natures, exercised through one person, would manifest both God and

* "Let us make man in our image, after our likeness."—*Gen.* i. 26. "Put on the new man, which is renewed in knowledge after the image of him that created him."—*Col.* iii. 10.

man. A perfect humanity being given, the Divine could then be seen elevated above human power, and yet in connection with it; * and the Divine love above, and yet in connection with human love.† The Divine prerogative, especially, could be exercised through the humanity, while yet the distinction between the human and the divine were clearly exhibited.‡ The Mediator would be man to the sense and God to the soul, and yet God to the soul through man to the sense.

HISTORICAL VERIFICATION.

In accordance with these deductions, the Son of God —the Mediator—was conceived of the Virgin Mary, by the power of the Holy Ghost. His humanity was thus, like the first Adam, created immediately by Divine energy, and was consequently free from transmitted evil, both of body and soul; and then, in this perfect humanity, "dwelled the fullness of the Godhead bodily." The Logos became flesh and dwelled among us,

* "He arose, and rebuked the winds and the sea; and there was a great calm."—*Matt.* viii. 26.

† "Greater love hath no man than this, that a man lay down his life for his friends."—*John*, xv. 13. "But God commendeth his love toward us, in that, while we were yet sinners, Christ died for us."—*Rom.* v. 8.

‡ "When Jesus saw their faith, he said unto the sick of the palsy, *Son, thy sins be forgiven thee.* But there were certain of the scribes sitting there, and reasoning in their hearts, Why doth this *man* thus speak blasphemies? who can forgive sins but *God* only?"—*Mark*, ii. 5–7.

and thus we receive the "light of the knowledge of the glory of God in the face of Jesus Christ."

The human and the divine were recognized in the person of Jesus by his disciples, and the doctrine lies in plain, intelligible phrase, upon the pages of the evangelists. With them Jesus ate and drank as a man; but he created food for the multitude as God. At the tomb of Lazarus he wept as a man; but he said, "Lazarus, come forth!" as a God. At his home in Nazareth he lived and loved as a man; upon his cross at Calvary he loved and died as a God. His agony testified of the man; the agony of nature testified of the God. He gave up the Ghost as a man; after the resurrection he breathed upon the disciples and said, "Receive ye the Holy Ghost," as a God. Thus, from the baptism to the ascension, power, and love, and prerogative, both human and divine, were manifested by that mysterious and yet comprehensible being, designated by Divine appointment—*God with us.*

So true to reason and history, and so perfectly adapted to the necessities of human character and condition, is the manifestation of God in Christ Jesus. The sum of the whole is, that, as a true knowledge of God is necessary in order to salvation from ignorance and sin, and as "no man hath seen God at any time"—"nor can any man know the Father except he to whomsoever the Son shall reveal him"—therefore, the only-begotten Son, who is in the bosom of the Father, hath revealed the moral character of the Divine Being to his creature, man. "*God was in Christ, reconciling the world unto himself, not imputing their trespasses unto them.*"

SUB-CHAPTER I.

LOVE FOR THE LAW-GIVER A SECOND SUBJECTIVE ELEMENT IN HUMAN SALVATION.

The character of the Law-giver being revealed, love for that character is necessary, in order that obedience may be acceptable to God and a blessing to man. *Truth is light, but love is life.* Truth in the precept is objective, in the sense that the perception of the duty imparts no inward moral power to fulfill the requirement. Love is subjective, in the sense that the recognition of the object of affection affects the subject, morally and vitally. A perception of the rectitude of the law, co-existing with love for the Law-giver, imparts both moral power and a moral blessing to the soul. Truth without love is like the sun in winter; it enlightens, but the heat is absent which cherishes life. Light without heat only reveals the deadness of the earth; it does not transform the desolation into forms of life and beauty. To know the character of the Law-giver is necessary, in order to guide us into the knowledge of duty. To love the Law-giver is necessary, before we can have spiritual happiness in obedience. Obedience prompted by knowledge of the precept is right; *but knowledge does not impart power to render such obedience.* Obedience guided by knowledge, and prompted by love, is *life and peace.* It is easy to perceive that without love for the Law-giver the soul could neither be happy in obedience, nor could the motive prompting obedience be acceptable with God. Nothing but an *appreciation* of the Divine character can produce obedience which is at the same time acceptable to the Divine Being and a conscious blessing to man. And it is proper here, for the sake of connection in the thought, to notice what will be amplified hereafter, *i. e.*, that love for the Law-giver can be generated only by the manifestation of the Law-giver's love for us. Love begets love; and, as things are constituted, in order that love may be generated in human bosoms, a manifestation of love on the part of the Divine Being is a necessary precedent.

SUB-CHAPTER II.

ADAPTATIONS IN THE MODE OF MANIFESTING DIVINE LOVE.

We have shown that the knowledge of God in Christ is manifested in a manner adapted to the constitution of the human mind. There may be not only a personal manifestation of God, but there are *modes* of manifestation which possess peculiarly-adapted power to affect human hearts. Truth may be exhibited by such methods, and in such relations, as greatly to augment its power *in* and *over* the human soul. That method which has power to awaken more than any other, the perceptive and appreciative powers of the human spirit, is the dramatic—a grouping of life-action, working in adapted scenery and circumstances, and imbued with the colors of deep emotion. There are in the human soul capabilities to do and to suffer which remain latent, unless developed by exigencies adapted to call out their power. Most men—perhaps every man—is conscious of the existence of such capabilities. When these dormant energies of the soul in others are awakened into life-action by extraordinary circumstances, and thus exhibited before the mind by perception or conception, the scene and the actors enchain the attention, and bring out a response from the depths of the human heart. It is in vain that one who reads the best delineations of Scott or Irving, or the "Uncle Tom" of Mrs. Beecher Stowe, says, "This is fiction, and I will not be affected by it as though it were fact." We may say, "This picture is an unreal creation of the fancy;" we may *know* that it is so, but we can not *feel* that it is so. Powers of the soul, deeper and stronger than the intellect, will answer the call when truth is personified and dramatized. Hence, when a public speaker illustrates his subject by life-anecdotes; when he says—"*He did it*," "*He suffered it*"—listless minds and wandering eyes are attracted, and memory treasures the illustration while she forgets the argument. Thus Jesus, the great Teacher, taught in parables; and "without a parable opened he not his mouth." There is recondite truth, which men should understand, involved in this characteristic of the human mind. The soul responds, because it sees a development of its own powers. If the scene which it contemplates is a truthful delineation of what a man can be, or do, or suffer, the soul will sympathize. When humanity is seen working under intense pressure, and thus developing the might of its faculties and affections in a crisis of trial and passion, then, as *like out of us awakens like in us*, so a presentation of intense life-action, clothed in the drapery of emotion, awakens a responsive echo through all the chambers of the human spirit.

There is a mode, then, of presenting truth which is more effective with the human mind than any other. That is when, by dramatic grouping, the generic capabilities of our nature for good or evil, to do or to endure, are developed in earnest action, wrought into the concrete before the eye of the soul. So we are made ; the actual and the possible, presented in a life-drama, has peculiar power over all the susceptibilities of the human mind.

This adapted mode being ascertained, the character of the Law-giver being revealed, and love for the Law-giver being necessary, and that love dependent upon a manifestation of Divine love—then, in order that the soul may be awakened and impressed in the mode adapted to move all its susceptibilities most deeply, *the Law-giver himself would personify love and obedience objectively, and intensify the effect by dramatic groupings of life-action and passion.* Thus, in a manner adapted to the constitution which the Maker has given us, would human attention be attracted, and the human faculties impressed by the great facts of redemption.

THE REQUIRED MODE ACTUALIZED IN THE LIFE-HISTORY AND LOVE-DEATH OF JESUS.

Reader, look with me and contemplate Christ's life of love and labor, culminating in the scenes of the garden, the judgment-hall, and the cross. The chief personage is divine. The love of the Godhead is seen exhibiting itself stronger than death. The holy city, the peculiar people, priests, Roman dignitaries, and bands of soldiers, are seen in the action of the moral spectacle. In the center is Calvary, where a cross is elevated in view of men and angels, and upon it the Divine Heart throbs in love-throes for the world. The sun pales, the earth shudders, the startled elements assume an impending scenic aspect, and become a dark back-ground, on which is displayed the moral miracle of Suffering Mercy. During the elemental gloom a hand is stretched out, which rends the temple vail, and shakes the fabric of the old dispensation to its center. The beholders are astonished and convicted.*

* Not only the ingenuous and truthful spirit of this narrative, but the *order of the facts*, which is evidently without design on the part of the narrators, in the points we shall notice, bears with it a strong confirmation of the *supernatural* occurrences mentioned in the text. When the Saviour of men is first elevated upon the cross, there are the contempt and mockery of the crowd. Elders, scribes, Jews, the passers-by, and the soldiers, all revile the Sufferer, and speak words of bitter derision and contumely. But after a short period elapses these same mockers, Gen-

The crisis of the death-agony has arrived. Jesus cries, "It is finished!" and gives up the ghost. * * * * * * The scene shifts. The powers of death and hell lie vanquished. Angels announce the triumph of the resurrection, at morning twilight, to women who are on a love-errand at the sepulcher. Incidents, solemn and soul-stirring, for a time intervene. The risen Redeemer commissions his disciples to preach the Gospel to all nations—promises the advent of the Holy

tile and Jew, experience a sudden change of conviction. "Surely this was the son of God!" said the centurion. "All the people," who are reported as mockers before the darkness and the earthquake, when they saw the things that were done, *smote their breasts*, and returned into the city. Joseph of Arimathea, belonging to a class who, even before the arrest of Jesus, were unwilling to be openly recognized as his disciples, goes boldly to Pilate, and asks the body of the crucified. Nicodemus, likewise, publicly aids to bury, in a manner testifying his reverence and respect, one whom in life he had visited in the night. Why this sudden change from contempt and mockery to consternation and penitence in the foes of Christ, while at the same time confidence is begotten in the hearts of his friends? The varied and diverse mental emotions given in this graphic narration are, by the laws of mind, the sequences of a sudden and profound change of mind in relation to the character of Jesus. There was no word or manifestation from Christ himself to produce this change. It can be accounted for in no other way than by assuming the supernatural phenomena as having occurred at the crisis marked in the narrative.

If the apostles were uninspired men, deceived themselves or desiring to deceive others, they could not have forged the facts, and then connected with them the legitimate mental sequences, as they have done. But every one who reads their several narrations will be convinced that the simple facts are recorded by the writers, without any apprehension on their part, of the natural and logical connection which they hold to the action and emotion subsequently described.

Ghost, and ascends from their presence to heaven——. Anon, the air is agitated as by mighty winds—the place is shaken where the chosen are assembled—the Holy Spirit descends—the symbol of its power and purity glows upon the heads of the apostles; they are conscious of the Divine energy, and commence the heaven-born *mission to conquer the world by* TRUTH *and* LOVE!

Thus the mode of manifestation is conformed to the human constitution. It impresses the facts of redemption upon the soul by a method adapted to accomplish the design. When the soul appreciates by faith this exhibition of God in Christ, the Divine love for man begets love in man for God. The affinity of affection which draws the soul to obedience is established between the Divine and the human minds. *The* LOVE-DEATH *of Christ, revealing through flesh, or the sensibility, the active benevolence of the Divine heart, communicates* LOVE-LIFE *to the souls of believers.* This new affection expels meaner ones, and begets new hopes and moral activity in the renewed mind. Those whom we love, and that which we hope for, we joyously labor for. The soul quickened by love, guided by knowledge, and sustained by hope, moves happily in the life of obedience. To the believer, God, in the love-sacrifice of Calvary, speaks with power, and speaks to all the faculties and susceptibilities of the human soul. The perverted and sleeping conscience is awakened and rectified. The heart answers in kind, "grace for grace." The will, as the resultant of our moral and rational nature * falls into subjection to the will of the Law-giver. Man is redeemed—recovered from rebellion and spiritual death, to serve the living God. Thus by adapted manifestations of the Divine character, and adapted modes of presenting those manifestations to the human mind, under the energy of the Divine Spirit, man is redeemed from ignorance and sin, and reconciled to God in Christ Jesus.

SUB-CHAPTER III.

CHRIST'S SACRIFICE IN ACCORDANCE WITH THE PROGRESS OF THINGS, THE NECESSITIES OF MAN, AND THE CHARACTER OF GOD.

ISAAC TAYLOR somewhere remarks, that the creation of man and the permission of sin may have implied on

* Ἐν ἑαυτοῖς κεκτήμενα τῆς μεταβόλης αἰτίαν:—"In themselves containing the cause of change:" *i. e.* The will is a resultant of changes produced within the circle of the individual consciousness by whatsoever those changes may be occasioned.—PLATO, *De Legibus*, lib. x.

So Cicero, *De Fato*, § 9. "Sic quum sine causa animum moveri decemus: sine externa causa moveri, non omnino sine causa decemus."

the part of the Creator the mission and sacrifice of Christ. This intimation is suggestive, especially when we consider that man, as a moral being, is placed in an imperfect physical world. It is probably true to the furthest extent, that those first facts implied all the series of remedial and redeeming agencies, from the creation of man to the close of human history. Progress is the method by which the Almighty works, not only in one department, but in all departments of creation. If Christ had not yet come, the analogy of nature, or rather the deductions of reason, founded upon what we now know of the work of creation, would teach the student of nature that a teacher of perfect morals would come. The transcendent intellect of Plato, in a darker age than the present, reached even to this conclusion.*

In accomplishing the plan by which God develops his character, and especially his essential attribute of benevolence, there was a remaining opportunity for a manifestation of Divine love more perfect than had been revealed before the time of Christ. God had not before the day of the crucifixion manifested fully and perfectly the strength of the Divine benevolence. He had not revealed all the love that *means*, *method*, and a Mediator could convey to man ; nor all that it was pos-

* Platonis Alcibiad. § ii.

sible for the human mind to appreciate. Love, especially in its temporal aspects, may be manifested by a benefactor without self-denials ; yet, the highest and holiest love can be revealed only by self-denial of one for the good of another.* It is self-denial in the flesh, or humanity, that affects humanity. In attracting and transforming the human heart the love-sacrifice is, beyond all question, the highest possible element of power. The human mind can appreciate Christ's sacrifice, but it can appreciate nothing more. Death upon the cross exhausted the capacity of man to invent means that would prolong and intensify death agonies. In addition to this utmost agony inflicted upon the body, Jesus suffered all that the power of malignant passion could inflict upon the mind, and all that sympathy for others could inflict upon the heart :—*his mother stood near the cross!* There is no mode, means, or medium, by which greater love could be manifested by self-denial ; and greater love the human heart has no power to appreciate, than that exhibited on the cross.

* Phil. of the Plan of Salvation, ch. xv.

"For what the law could not do, in that it was weak through the flesh, God, sending his own Son in the likeness of sinful flesh, and by a sacrifice for sin condemned sin in the flesh, that the righteousness of the law might be fulfilled in us, who walk not after the flesh but after the Spirit."—*Rom.* viii. 3, 4.

Before the sacrifice of Christ, then, there was a place for the fuller and stronger manifestations of Divine love for man; since the sacrifice of Jesus no possibility remains of revealing to humanity, in its present condition, greater love than that manifested in the crucifixion. The precept, the example, and the manifestation of Divine love, are all perfected in Jesus. Without God in Christ the revelation of the Divine nature would not have been complete. The manifestation of love would not be perfect and infinite. With it the ultimate revelation of the Divine nature develops the ultimate capabilities of the human soul. Thus the *truth is sealed* beyond further development in the present state, because this ultimate manifestation of God is adequate to accomplish the *ultimate* development of the moral nature of man.

THE MANIFESTATION OF LOVE IN THE SACRIFICE OF CHRIST ESSENTIAL TO THE HIGHEST GOOD OF MAN.

The more of pure affection for God and man there is in the world, the more elevated and happy will be the condition of mankind. But the sum of love in human bosoms, as we have seen, can be increased only by a manifestation of Divine love for human beings. Man can love God no further than he has faith that "God is love." As the first seed of things are from God, and every seed begets its kind, hence the love of God, revealed in the sacrifice of Christ, is the seed which, planted by faith and vivified by the Holy Spirit, begets charity in the human soul. Hence, if man is restored to obedience to the law, which requires him to love God with all his heart and his neighbor as himself, it must be by an influx of love from the Divine heart into the human heart. The Divine nature can only be truly known to the consciousness of man by a revelation of love. It is not by precept alone, but by manifestation that God is known to the soul. "*God is love.*"—"*He that loveth is born of God.*"—"*He that loveth not, knoweth not God; for God is love.*"—"*We love God, because he first loved us.*" A new influx of love from the Divine heart was, therefore, the alone means by which man could be blessed and elevated beyond former conditions. And as, previously to the sacrifice of Christ, the love of God was revealed only in shadows, not in substance, nor in perfection, hence the progress and perfection of the scheme of revelation, as well as the necessities of human nature, implied the final manifestation of the Divine nature in the sacrifice of Calvary.

SUCH A MANIFESTATION INFERRED FROM THE CHARACTER OF GOD.

"God is love," and Divine love would, from its nature, seek manifestation; because a manifestation of love does good, and *love in the nature seeks good as its end.* And as, in the economy of revelation, there was a place for the introduction of more love-power among men, both the plan of God and the nature of God would lead him to fill that place and offer that sacrifice. Thus the fitness of things—the necessities of man's moral nature, and the character of God are filled and fulfilled in the sacrifice of Christ.

CHAPTER VI.

THE ADAPTATION AND PROCESS OF THE GOSPEL IN RESTORING MAN TO IMPARTIAL REGARD FOR HIS FELLOW-MAN, THUS PRODUCING AFFECTIONATE OBEDIENCE TO THE SECOND TABLE OF THE LAW.

We have shown that love is the element out of which springs acceptable obedience to God, and we have exhibited the process by which man is restored to conformity to the *first table* of the law—*supreme love to the Law-giver.* But the divine law requires that we should not only love God supremely, but our neighbor as ourself.

Man is created an active being, a free moral agent; but his *active powers* can be developed only under the second table of the law—obedience to God is labor for man. The agency energized by love constitutes the life of righteousness required by the divine law. Now, as God needs no active agency on the part of man in order to promote His good; as the will of man can be developed into love-action only under the second table of the law; and as it is here alone that man can glorify God by promoting that love and obedience which is demanded by the moral law—we inquire whether the manifestation of God in Christ provides for the restoration of the human soul to *equal love* for man, and to *love-action* in his behalf?

PRELIMINARY PRINCIPLES STATED.

Both natural and revealed religion teach that assimilation to the character of God—subjection of the human to the Supreme will—is the ultimate duty of man; and the prevailing religions of mankind in times past and present have reached, without much variation, this ultimate conception. This is especially true wherever time and circumstances have favored a philosophical development of any religious system.* In all such in-

* The Oriental theosophies, which reached full development before or about the time of Christ, all contained the idea of acquiescence in the Supreme will as the ultimate good of man. The Gnostic sought acquiescence in the Divine will as the supreme good. With them, to rise above earthly affections and desires, and attain to a union with the Pleroma, was the end of science (gnosis).

In Plato, who reached the ultimate in the development of spiritualism among the Greeks, there is the analogue of the Oriental and Gnostic philosophies. The lowest love in Plato's theology is sensual; the second, complex, or sensuo-rational; the highest, the love of the Absolute Good. To rise above the agitations produced by matter and sense, and attain to the knowledge and love of the Supreme True and Good, was the aim of reason and the end of life.

So, too, the Hindoo system of the Vedas, still prevalent in the East. The disciple, according to the Vedanta exposition of Budhism, must lose

stances human reason reaches the ultimate conception, that the final end and duty of the soul is submission of the will—consecration of the self to the Supreme Di-

his own will, separate himself from sense, and retire into himself by reflection. He learns, then, that Brahma alone exists—every thing else is illusion. To lose the individual will in Brahma, and become quiescent in the contemplation of him, is the highest attainment. Budhism, according to the missionary Medhurst, is developed to this ultimate conception in China. And in Siam, according to the statements of Dr. Bradley, the idea of quiescence in the Divine will is carried even to the supposition that conscious identity is annihilated.

The religion of Mohammed includes the same idea as its nucleus. *Islamism* is the devotion of self to the supreme will of God. This, as the word signifies, is the final end of the Mohammedan ritual. In all sects professing the religion of the Koran, *Islam*, or conformity to Allah, is distinctly developed as the "sum of piety."

In examining the ground-forms of these systems, we do not always find a dogma at the beginning which enjoins self-consecration of the worshiper to the Supreme of his system; but as all religions must assume that God is supreme and man a dependent subject, the reason develops unfailingly (shall we say, constitutionally?) the final exposition that the finite finds its highest good in assimilation to the will of the Infinite.

But as God in no system of natural religion is conceived of as denying himself for human good, hence the human will can be brought to this benevolent activity only by faith in Christ.

The philosophers of the most enlightened age of Greece seem generally to have adopted the same opinion. Aristotle, in his Ethics, argues from the nature of the gods that happiness consists in abstract contemplation, even in a contemplation by which no moral action was developed. Thus the philosophies and the religions which are the product of the unaided reason agree in a tenet which is antagonistic to human progress, and to the active virtues which Christianity and the moral wants of human nature require.

Aristotle in his *Ethics*, book x. ch. viii., thinks that good men, being members of society, will act virtuously, because they *must act* from the necessity of their circumstances; yet he says, "that perfect happiness is vinity. But if the character of that Divinity, if the will of the Supreme, be not active benevolence for man as a family, the human will, by consecration, does not become benevolent. The inert, or selfish, or malignant character of the object to which the will is consecrated, paralyzes or perverts the human powers, instead of developing them into active obedience to the second table of the law.

But in order to fulfill the second table of the law, the act of the will must originate in love to man; in love to man as a being; in love to the true character of man, as God created him. We are prepared now to inquire whether faith in Christ produces love for man, and whether submission of the will to Christ produces love-action for the good of man?

a kind of contemplative happiness might be shown from hence, that we suppose the gods to be pre-eminently blessed and happy. But what moral acts can we attribute to them?—Shall they be acts of justice? Would they not appear ridiculous making bargains, or restoring deposits, or such-like acts? Or shall we attribute to them courageous actions that they may undertake formidable things, or meet dangers, because this would be honorable? Or shall we attribute to them benevolent actions?—but to whom shall they give? * * * Even if they are temperate, what would follow?—Is not praise absurd, because they have no bad desires? *And if we went through every case of moral action they would seem small and unworthy of gods.* Yet all suppose that they live and cogitate, for they do not sleep like Endymion. To him, therefore, *who lives, but is abstracted from moral action,* and still more so from production, what is left but contemplation? So that the energy of the Divine Being, as it exceeds in blessedness, must be contemplative: *and therefore, of human energies that which is nearest allied to this must be the happiest.*"

BY FAITH IN CHRIST WE LOVE BOTH THE TRUE GOD AND THE TRUE MAN AT THE SAME TIME.

We have spoken of the fact that in Christ a true humanity was revealed in union with the Divinity, but we have not exhibited the reasons and relations of this merciful revelation of the true human nature.

It was not only necessary that the character of God should be revealed, in order that man might love the true God, but it was likewise *necessary that the true character of man should be revealed, in order that man might love the true man.* Christ was both the true God and the true man. In him God was manifested *as he is,* and *man was manifested as he should be.* Our race had lost the knowledge of the true man as certainly and as hopelessly as they had lost the knowledge of the true God. By faith in Christ we believe both in the true God and the true man at the same time. *He, therefore, who loves Christ, loves both the true God and the true man* IN HIM. *Faith in Christ works by love to man as he should be, and by labor to make man what he should be.*

Now, if we love the true humanity in Christ, we will love it every where. *Humanity in Christ is generic.* It is the second Adam; the impersonation of man as

God created him; the true soul, faculties, and susceptibilities of the being, MAN.

God and man being thus united in Christ, it is not possible to love God in Christ without loving man in Christ at the same time. Thus the manifestation of God in Christ produces in the human soul love for both God and man. *It brings the soul into conformity with both divisions of the law.* "He therefore who saith, I love God, and hateth his brother, is a liar."* His brother that he hath seen is in his nature, although sin-marred in character, a living type of the humanity of Jesus. The true humanity is a finite moral image of the infinite God. In kind, but not in degree of excellence or power, the *perfect moral nature* of man is a created image of the divine. He, therefore, who loveth not his brother whom he hath seen, loves not the true God whom he hath not seen. But every one who is assimilated by faith to the character and will of Christ, loves both the true God and the true man, in him, at the same time.

THE PRACTICAL OPERATION OF THESE PRINCIPLES. FAITH IN CHRIST'S SACRIFICE PRODUCES LOVE—FAITH IN HIS LIFE PRODUCES ACTION.

We come now to the practical application of these foundation principles of the Gospel:—Christ being

* 1 John, iv. 20.

recognized and loved as the Supreme, what character and conduct would be the product of the consecration of the will to Him ?

No one doubts but that love for Christ is the true motive power of the Gospel. This is assented to by all Protestant denominations, and by all benevolent associations that labor to enlighten and save men. We will, therefore, assume here what we have proved before, that the motive power in all Gospel effort is the love of Christ, and proceed to show how faith, which works by love, guides men into that benevolent activity of which the self-denial of Christ for human good is both the motive and the model.

CHRIST THE MODEL-MAN. FAITH IN HIS LIFE PRODUCES BENEVOLENT ACTION FOR HUMAN GOOD.

Love for Christ as the true man produces labor to make others like Christ. The character of Jesus is the standard to which the believer aspires, and to which he will labor to bring others. The love of Christ makes him the model into which Christians labor to fashion the human character. There are men destitute of living faith in Christ, who are, no doubt, sincerely endeavoring to benefit their fellow-men, and whatever character may be the model of excellence with any such class of men, they will endeavor to mold society into that form. Love for a model character must, by the laws of mind, produce this effect. *If we love those for whom we labor, we will labor to make them like those whom we love.* A man whose ideal of excellence is some distinguished statesman, if he love no standard more than this, will desire that his son should attain to the same excellency. So when the ideal model is a successful director of monetary or military affairs, the father or friend will endeavor to conform those he loves best to that standard, if the attainment of the character be within the limit of hopeful ambition. So there are ideal conditions, in which men of good intentions seek the happiness of society. Some would have all in communities, seeking their chief good in equal worldly condition.* Other philanthropists seek the chief good

* Such men as Owen of Lanark, and Horace Greely of New York, possessing apparently a natural good will for man, which we sometimes see exhibited both in ancient and modern times, have labored long, and expended large amounts of money, to perfect the scheme of social communities. But such schemes must forever fail to produce happiness, or gain the ends desired. The individuals are brought together in all such instances by selfishness. In the communal arrangement each seeks his supreme good. But the aggregation of selfish individuals can not produce benevolence. Selfish action and self-seeking only confirm a selfish disposition, and the accumulation of selfishness in such associations will, in the end, produce an explosion, which will scatter the fragments again into common society. In the United States this has already been the result in many cases. This was the result of Owen's effort on the Wabash, in the State of Indiana. Society might be benefited, and social comfort and usefulness produced, in some cases, by association. With the Chris-

of men in some new arrangement of the social economy. Among men who are not influenced by faith in Christ, which makes Him the standard of human excellence, plans to attain the good of man as an individual are as various as they were in the days of the Greek sages, of whom Varro writes that they sought the chief good in a multitude of diverse conditions. Without love for Christ there can be no unanimity among men in their efforts to promote human welfare. All who reject the Christian faith, and depend for ultimate good on objective conditions, make the radical mistake of supposing that man's chief good consists in objective attainments, not in subjective exercises. To seek the chief good in any object that does not produce love and purity within us, is to destroy the peace for which we seek. As the man who drinks of a poisoned fountain, the more he drinks the more he thirsts, so is the fool who endeavors to satisfy his spiritual

tian principle, as it exists in Moravian communities, where love for Christ produces labor for man as the primary object of life, associated labor is happy and successful labor, because it is a labor of love. It satisfies conscience, relieves men of all sense of danger regarding the comfortable maintenance of self and children, takes away temptations to self-aggrandizement, and aids social enjoyment; while at the same time the laborer every day enjoys the hope of future blessedness, and if self-denials are to be made, they are made for Christ's sake. Thus selfishness is restrained, from marring the bonds which unite the society, and its power over the minds of individuals is abated, because the action and the aim is directed, not for self as an end, but for Christ and humanity.

wants by temporary aliment.* Social arrangements and temporal acquisitions may be auxiliaries to happiness in the case of those who have purifying love in their hearts, but these, without subjective benevolence, can not give life or happiness. Men might raise a suffering mendicant as high as temporal acquisition could elevate him, while still his happiness would be less and his influence worse. The highest good of man consists in that state of mind in which his action is prompted by love. To bring men into the *life of love,* so that they will act in accordance with the *law of love,* is to accomplish the end in which alone the nature of the soul, and the laws of the moral universe, will allow man to find his chief good. Now, Jesus Christ is the model of this attainment, both in character and action, hence the love of Christ is the only impulse that both moves and guides the soul in right action for the good of man.†

* "Thou fool, this night thy soul shall be required of thee." "This night" of the soul, when in its moral darkness it endeavors to satisfy itself by temporal acquisitions.

† Do we, then, discard the efforts of those who, while they are without faith in Christ, labor to promote human interests? By no means! We desire neither to discard nor discredit such efforts. One of the highest instincts of living beings is sympathy with the wronged and the suffering. Even in the orders of animals below man, the cry of distress will arouse creatures of the same species, and bring them to the rescue of the suffering one. The philanthropist who obeys the highest instinct of our nature, and rallies to the rescue of the wronged or the needy, evinces nobility of nature far beyond those who, while they may profess to love

THE LOVE OF CHRIST PRODUCES LOVE TO MAN AS A GENUS.

Another characteristic development of the human soul produced by love to Christ is, that those who possess it will oppose EVERY THING which injures man. Christians love man for the sake of his nature—his true nature, as revealed in the Mediator. *It is the love of humanity*, not the love of some single attribute or condition of humanity; the love of humanity, *in itself considered*, not the love of one race or class of the human family.

Now, an individual who loves man *as man*, will oppose every thing which degrades his character, abates his happiness, or impairs his rights. A Christian father loves his son—that son is beset by several evils; one man aims to lead him into vice, another to make him a slave, another to keep him in mental error or personal degradation—the father will not only oppose one, but all of these; and the opposition of the parent will be strong in proportion to the magnitude of the evil sought to be inflicted upon the object of his affection. This is the very nature of love; a person who loves another

Christ, deny by their conduct both the higher instincts of humanity and the holier impulses of divine love in the heart. Love for the true Christ gives divine life to the natural instinct, and rightly directs human efforts for human good.

can not do otherwise than oppose every thing which injures the person or the interests of the loved object. And not only in relation to all evils, but a father will do so in relation to *all his children*. If he feel thus toward one and not toward another, he has lost the true instincts of a parent's heart. If he is very hostile to one influence which would injure his child, while he is willing he should be injured by some other, his mind is blinded or perverted. Love, in its nature and its development, is opposed to every thing that will injure the object of affection. Such love for man faith in Christ begets in the human soul. The Christian loves man as man; wherever, therefore, there is a human nature, he will oppose every thing that mars the attributes or defiles the susceptibilities of that nature. A man who loves Christ loves every man, because every man bears the image of that humanity which he loves in the person of the Mediator. The image is marred, indeed, in its moral features; hence, as we have shown, love will produce labor to redeem the fallen and restore the true humanity.

The love of Christ, therefore, produces effort for human good that is "without partiality and without hypocrisy." The true friend of man can not be opposed to war and at the same time tolerate slavery; he can not oppose slavery while he knowingly encourages or perpetrates other wrongs which degrade or injure men. In whatever heart love to the true Christ lives, opposition to every thing which wrongs or defiles man is one of its *natural* developments. Christ recognizes human nature *as His nature*, and the principle is incorporated into the phraseology of that decree which settles the final destiny of the soul—"Inasmuch as ye did it unto one of the least of these *my brethren*, ye did it unto me."

LOVE FOR HUMANITY AS REVEALED IN CHRIST PRODUCES EFFORT FOR THE VARIOUS CLASSES AND CONDITIONS OF MEN IN PROPORTION TO THEIR NEED.

A third characteristic development of the love which is produced by faith in Christ is, that it leads men to labor first and most for those who most need sympathy and effort. This is so plain a characteristic of divine love—it is exhibited so fully in the character and teachings of Christ, that it is a matter of wonder that many in all ages, professing regard for the Gospel, have misconceived or overlooked this characteristic action of a benevolent will.

It is the nature of love that it develops itself for its objects without partiality and without hypocrisy. A mother has a family of children; she loves all her offspring alike; but one is suffering and in danger, and therefore needs her assistance more than others. What will that mother do? Will she administer to others while she neglects the suffering one? Not if she has a mother's heart. A mother will leave those who need her care less and go to befriend and succor those in want of sympathy or assistance. True love can do nothing else. That love is partial or impure that does not distribute to its objects in proportion to their measure of want. If the love of humanity, as a nature, dwell in our hearts when one class of men need effort in their behalf more than others, Christian love directs effort to the more needy. This is the nature of true love, both human and divine, and the one is illustrated by the other.

To guide the human mind into unselfish and unsectarian effort for human good, the Saviour has presented truth in varied and striking forms. When the disciples of John came in their master's name to inquire whether Jesus were the Messiah, he replied—"Go, tell John that I bestow temporal benefits first upon those who are most needy: the *poor*—the *sick*—the *blind!* and so I do spiritually; *the poor have the Gospel preached unto them.*" John knew the characteristics of Divine Love. The message settled the question: and that *Voice* which reproved sin in high places, prob-

11

ably exulted in the confirmation of its utterances before it was hushed by the ax of the executioner.

A Jew, professing to love God, and who assented to the sum of the divine law, asked Jesus—"Who is my neighbor?" In answer we have the striking parable of the man who fell among thieves. Some who professed to teach the prevailing religion passed by the helpless sufferer, while yet relief was granted by one whom the Pharisees supposed to be an alien from the true faith, and who was not, probably, so orthodox in theory as themselves. Jesus approved the conduct of the Samaritan—sanctioned it for all time as an illustration of true neighborship; and commanded the inquirer to "go and do likewise."

Superadded we have the parables of the lost sheep and the lost piece of money. The true shepherd will leave the ninety-and-nine who are in less danger, to succor the one exposed to the wolf and beasts of prey. The import of this teaching can not be doubted; that alone is moral love for man which produces labor *first* and *most* for those in greatest need of sympathy and succor.

This moral love for man, which fulfills the second table of the law, is exemplified and illustrated by the life of the Son of God, and by all the apostles and evangelists and martyrs of Christ, whose history is referred to in the New Testament. The higher reason and the influence of the Divine Spirit in the heart likewise teach this doctrine. The truth of the statement is beyond controversy, that with those who have faith in the true man as revealed in Christ, love rises and urges in proportion to the wrongs and helplessness of men. This characteristic needs not to be argued with the Christian's heart. Jesus left the bosom of the Father—he left the adoring presence of obedient spirits, and *came to seek and to save those who were lost.* And every one whose will is assimilated to that of Christ will go and do likewise. Thus the active moral powers of the soul, which are paralyzed or perverted by a false faith, find their ultimate and true development by faith in Christ—a development which harmonizes the will of the believer with the plan and labor of Christ in saving lost men.

The conclusion, then, we think, is fairly gained, that the revelation of the human nature in connection with the divine nature in Christ consecrates the will of those who love Jesus to the glory of God in the good of men. The spirit and the example of the true man as exhibited in the life of Christ—*the authority which the divine gives to the human by the connection of the two;* and added to these, the weightiest sanction by which human duty can be enforced—the sanction of the judgment, in which Christ identifies himself with the wronged and suffering classes of men, recognizes his own nature in them, and receives acts done for them as done for him, and to him: all these unite to develop the will of man into love—labor for human good, and to confirm the soul in benevolent obedience.

Thus does the manifestation of the true God and the true man in Christ mold the moral powers of our nature into the character of active benevolence which is required by the law—it meets the ultimate demand of the human reason, and transforms the satisfied and sanctified human spirit into the image of the Redeemer.

CHAPTER VII.

THE MANIFESTATION OF GOD IN CHRIST, CONSIDERED IN ITS RELATIONS TO THE FUTURE LIFE.

We have noticed the possibility and the method of redemption, and the final issue in the development of a benevolent will; and we have shown that law can not be broken, even for mercy's sake. We will notice now, finally, the manner in which mercy is administered in adaptation to the mental constitution of man, as a being destined to exist during the present and the future life.

THE OPPOSITE POLES OF THE AFFECTIONS.

We can not love two things of opposite characters at the same time: to whichsoever a man determines, he will, as he grows in love to one, become opposed to the other.* Love and hatred are the opposite poles of the affections. One can not exist without its antagonism;

* "If he love the one he will hate the other: ye can not serve God and Mammon."—*Jesus.*

therefore, where love to one character exists, alienation from the opposite character exists necessarily. This is law in the moral world—this the nature of moral beings.

It is likewise a law, governing both our physical and mental economy, that each faculty is strengthened by exercise, while the non-use or misuse paralyzes or perverts both the physical and moral faculties. As the action of one arm and the non-action of the other will develop the one and paralyze the other, so mental habits of one moral character, strengthen the disposition to act in that direction and destroy the disposition to act in a different one. The moral powers, by their own exercise, strengthen themselves to act in the chosen direction, while they lose strength to act in the opposite. Jesus spoke according to these laws—He that increased his talent by proper use, received the reward of ten pounds. He that paralyzed his ability to do good by disuse or abuse, received the sentence—"Take from him his talent." "Whosoever hath, to him shall be given; and whosoever hath not, even that which he hath shall be taken from him."*

* Matt. xxv. 28, 29.

THE NATURAL ACTION OF THE MIND CONFIRMS A WORLDLY AND SELFISH CHARACTER.

The mind is an ever-active being; and human happiness, as we have shown, depends upon the right exercise of the moral faculties. But by nature every man's faculties are first exercised by the things of the earth. The objects of the earth first attract our attention and develop our affections. We do not inquire here, why men are in their present moral condition. "That which is born of the flesh is flesh." To the fact, so far as it is necessary in our argument, all men will assent. The affections and will are first attached to, and exercised by, earthly objects.

This attachment to earthly objects "grows with our growth and strengthens with our strength." Thus the natural exercises of the mind tend to confirm a selfish and unsatisfied spirit—selfish, because earthly ends are sought from supreme love to ourselves; and unsatisfied, because the aliment is not adapted to the want. The appetite for bread can not be satisfied with "a stone." It is absurd to suppose that temporal good will satisfy spiritual wants.

THE PENALTY INDUCED BY SUPREME ATTACHMENT TO EARTHLY OBJECTS.

Although the objects of the world can not satisfy those who seek them as their chief good, yet to separate worldly minds from the objects of their love renders them miserable. The heart will ache and bleed when it is separated from the objects of its supreme regard: "It is home where'er the heart is." The principle is fundamental and unfailing—"where the treasure is, there will the heart be also."

Now the objects which are loved supremely on earth can not be transferred into a future state. When a man dies, he must, from the nature of the case, either lose or gain happiness by the transition. If the objects of his supreme affection are on earth, he leaves them; if they are in the spiritual world, he goes to them. Those who loved the objects of earth supremely will be separated from their idols. The transient and unsatisfying gratification which they afforded by self-elevation or sensuous enjoyment must cease. The selfish spirit must enter the next life with desolated affections, and a disposition confirmed in aversion to spiritual and holy things. The man who fails of the grace to love God supremely and man impartially, loses his highest good by violating the highest law. While here, he was unsatisfied in possessing earthly good; and there his soul is desolate, being separated from objects which he most desired.

ANOTHER ASPECT OF THE PENALTY CONSEQUENT UPON PERVERTED AFFECTIONS.

The supreme love of earthly good not only confirms the soul in selfishness, but it engenders and strengthens evil passions. When earthly objects are supreme with the mind, they are sought for the sake of self. Thus the whole action of the life tends to confirm selfishness in those who seek their chief good on earth. Self is the motive, and self, in some relation, the end of their activity. But minds thus confirmed in selfishness must, from the nature of the case, in seeking self-elevation or self-gratification, come into conflict with each other. And whenever the selfishness of one being, in pursuit of selfish ends, hinders or defeats another, evil passions will rise to agitate and curse the mind. Thus, by violating the law of God, which requires supreme love for the Supreme Being, and equal love for man, the soul works out for itself dire unrest in this world, and secures for itself the curse of a selfish heart, possessed by evil passions in the world to come. *To love God and man is positive good in the soul;* to love self more than these violates the supreme moral law, and engenders hell in human hearts.

INTERWORKING OF THE GOSPEL WITH THE LAWS OF MIND.

How, now, is the Gospel adapted to save the soul from its natural affections and tendencies, and induce, in their stead, the elements of heaven? The general answer to this inquiry is obvious: in view of the principles before stated, the Gospel adaptation would be found in such manifestations and methods of grace as are fitted to transfer the affections from earthly to heavenly objects. In this condition alone the soul finds life. Is, then, the Gospel mercy, in its process and its power, adapted to transfer supreme affection from earthly to heavenly objects, and to do this in accordance with the laws of mind?

We have already noticed the generative nature of love, and that the love of God in Christ is so manifested as to produce in human hearts love for the Lawgiver. We have noticed that the method of the manifestation is the one best adapted to awaken and enliven all the powers of the human soul. In these particulars, the means and the methods by which they are applied are adapted to attract the affections from the objects of earth, and attach them to the objects of heaven.

We desire here to exhibit the same subject in other views, which relate more particularly to the transition of the soul from the scenes of the present to those of the future state.

In order that the dwellers in this world may love the objects of the spiritual world, those objects must be manifested to us on earth. Man, as a mortal, is an earthly being. He is localized on the earth. His affections, as we have noticed, naturally seek their objects of attachment in the earth. We are so constituted and so located that an object must approach us in order that the susceptibilities may be affected by its excellency or its power. In order, therefore, that men may become attached to the objects and principles of the kingdom of heaven, the kingdom of heaven must "come nigh unto us."

Now, these *local necessities* of men are met by the revealment of the kingdom of heaven in the person and precepts of Christ. The King of the heavenly world, the objects which should be supremely loved, come down to earth, and act in connection with the living scenes and interests of humanity. Jesus exhibits to men the inferior character of earthly things, and reveals, in contrast with these, his own spiritual excellences, and the value of spiritual blessings. The objects of heaven live on the earth in the presence of men.

The laws of the "kingdom of God"—those which prevail beyond the grave—the spirit of the angelic spheres—that which moves the affections of all loyal subjects of the Divine government, are here—*all are here—with men—on earth—in time.*

These objects being revealed on earth in man's home, are thus presented before the mind in contrast with those earthly things which seek our supreme regard. By this method of mercy, the individual, whose affections had been drawn to the things of earth as his chief good, is met in the same earthly circumstances by the spiritual objects which should be supreme in his soul. They are so presented that the eye of faith is invited to perceive the glories of the Saviour. The sympathies of the Mediator's flesh is adapted to attract human sympathy—the affinities are brought near that they may affect each other. And then the fingers of mercy, energized by Divine influence, untwine the tendrils of the heart from their inordinate attachment to perishable objects, and the spiritualized affections tremble toward Jesus, as the magnetized needle trembles to the pole.

Thus, by the revealment on earth of the objects of heaven, by the human sympathies through which they are administered, the objects of heaven attract the affections of believers on earth. The treasure of the soul is then no longer with earthly objects, but with heavenly objects. Thus the life is hid with Christ in God. The new affection is now supreme in the human soul. Earthly attachments may exist, but they are subordinated in the soul's estimation to those which are spiritual. The pressure of selfish objects continues upon the affections; but they now become a temptation, which often give the soul trial and solicitude, where before they were the supreme attraction.

Now it must, we think, be apparent to the reason of every one, that when such a mind leaves the earth, it leaves solicitudes and trials to find blessedness in approaching into nearer communion with the objects of its affections. Its treasure, while on earth, was in heaven; it therefore leaves the earth to obtain its treasure; "It is home where'er the heart is:" the sanctified heart, even while on earth, is with its treasure in heaven;—to die, therefore, is to go home:

> "Then welcome death; thy freezing kiss
> Emancipates—the rest is bliss."

JOY OF THE RIGHTEOUS IN CONNECTION WITH THE PRINCIPLE OF PROGRESS.

We have noticed the considerations which teach that the method of Divine government includes the principle of moral progress. By faith in Christ progress in moral good becomes an element of happiness to the soul. The soul rejoices in the advancement of interests in which its affections are engaged. All benevolent minds find their happiness increased by the advancement of moral purity and moral principles on the earth. The "angels rejoice over one sinner that repenteth." The repentance of each individual that returns to obedience is an advance of good in the moral government of God. The principle of progress secures constant gratification to all who are interested by faith in the person and plans of the Redeemer. Now the kingdom of Christ is established upon the earth among men, and the advancement of its interests engage the sympathy and efforts of all who love the Lord. Thus, in the present life, the interests of the Christian heart are linked with moral progress in the government of God. The advance, therefore, of moral interests in the world becomes a spiritual blessing to the Christian mind. The principle of progress in the government of God thus provides a perpetual source of joy for all who love the reign of Christ.

The Scriptures exhibit this truth directly and by implication. They speak of Christians as being in sympathy with the progress of Christ's kingdom—they represent the spirits of the just as interested in the development of the plan of salvation upon the earth,* and angels as ministering spirits find their joy in moral progress. The mysterious utterances of the Apocalypse are, at least, intelligible upon this point. As the Lord of lords goes forth by his truth, providence, and spirit, conquering and to conquer, at every new conquest achieved by truth and love, the friends of the Lamb in heaven and upon earth worship and utter demonstrations of joy and triumph. Their sympathies are with the progress of truth, and as the Gospel triumphs over error and selfishness, they are exhilarated and blessed.

Now the man whose soul is awakened and identified in will and sympathy with the Prince and the principle of progress, is linked in with a law that will secure his interests and produce joy in the future life. It is probable that the principle of progress prevails throughout the moral universe. It is certain that it prevails in this world, to which human spirits belong, and in which those who love Christ become engaged in the advance of moral interests. Hence in this life, but more especially in the next, the knowledge that the power of God is exerted to advance moral good will produce worship, and the fact of advance will produce joy. As the triumphs of moral power go on—as the Papacy

* Luke, ix. 30, 31. Revelation, xxii. 9.

rocks and struggles to its fall—as slavery is abated and abolished—as light penetrates the dark places of the earth—as individual transgressors repent and return to obedience, the soul in sympathy with moral progress will triumph in the triumphs of moral power—and the spontaneous utterances of the heart will be "Alleluiah! for the Lord God omnipotent reigneth."

"Exult, ye saints!—ye can not fail;
Your destiny ye bind
To that supreme, eternal law,
Which rules the march of mind.
As God still lives, and as the soul
Is his undying breath,
Ye shall exult when hoary wrongs
Are smitten unto death."

Thus the constitution of man's moral nature harmonizes with the principle of progress in the moral creation, and whosoever is restored to harmony with the laws of the moral universe, finds here and hereafter in the principle of moral progression a source of unfailing interest and joy.

THE INTERNAL AND EXTERNAL LIFE.—EXPOSITION OF THE PRINCIPLE.

The connection between the present and future state is constituted not only in harmony with the laws of the affections, as we have seen, but likewise in harmony with the laws of the intelligence. The impressions made upon our senses by outward objects, and the thoughts which are originated by these, are the furniture of the mind and the treasure of the memory. The spirit lives in itself by digestion, or by reflection upon first thought, furnished by sensation. Then, by a law of the mind, reflection brings the object that first awakened the perception into the presence of the soul. By faith spiritual objects make an impression upon the internal life, as outward objects do upon the senses. What the objects and action of temporal phenomena are to the sensuous man, spiritual objects recognized by faith are to the spiritual man. If a man be shut up in a prison whose mind lives upon the objects of the external world, when the prison-door is closed he is separated from his chief good; the consequence is, a bereaved and unhappy mind. He must then live by reflection. If he deserve his doom, reflection will make him unhappy. And if he does not deserve it, reflection will still make him unhappy, because his soul will feed on his own sin or the sins of others. But if the chief love of the soul be spiritual, then by reflection the object of love will be present in the soul, and the presence of a chief love always produces happiness. Those who love Christ can not be imprisoned for known crime, and if they suffer wrongfully they can "rejoice and be exceeding glad," because in their trial they have the promise, and are conscious of the presence and favor of the chiefest object of their affection. The love of their soul is spiritual, not local and temporal. Bolts and chains can not exclude spiritual objects,* faith makes them a present entity to the mind.

In furnishing the mind for immortality, then, those objects which are spiritual should be treasured as the chief good of the soul. The time is coming when every mind must live by reflection. Then, the aliment upon which it lives will be either temporal or spiritual things, according as it has chosen its chief good. If Christ be enthroned in the affections, reflection upon his life of merciful labor, his self-sacrifice made in love, his lordship in providence, and by his Spirit, as he rules and furthers the moral progress of the universe—these will furnish, in the immortal state, perpetual aliment for the affections, and perpetual exercise for the intelligence, in analytic and synthetic combinations of the great facts in the scheme of mercy developed in the government of which Christ is the Mediator and the Administrator.

* Acts, xvi. 25: "And at midnight Paul and Silas prayed and sang praises." See also *Histories of the Persecuted in all Ages.*

THE CONNECTION OF THE PRESENT AND FUTURE STATE, AS CONSTITUTED BY THE LAW OF SUGGESTION.

The law of suggestion, or association of ideas, is a governing law of the intelligence. Without it there is no conscious identity, no logical memory, no ratiocination. There can be no such thing as a sane mind devoid of this law. The law of cause and effect rules as really in the mental as it does in the external phenomenal world. So long as consciousness and memory last, the law of suggestion will rule the intelligence, and an experience in the soul of the effects of past acts of life will bind the mind to a consideration of the cause which produced those effects.

Now we have shown that a soul whose chief treasure is on earth will feel a sense of evil and deprivation when removed from the things of sense. This mental woe must suggest the cause which produced it—the acts of a selfish and sinful life. The consequences of sins felt in the soul will suggest the sins which caused the evil effects which the soul experiences. Thus the mind will be doomed, by its own laws, to live in the presence of its own sin. God's laws are self-executed. The circle of unhallowed suggestion is formed by the voluntary sins of life. The circle is closed by natural death. In this world the consequence of sin is often separated from its cause by the interposition of sensuous objects, and by the arrangements of a probationary condition. In the world of reflection, and by the laws of reflection, sin and its consequences are united. The sins of life, by confirming earthly affections and evil habits, unite in a product of spiritual evil in the soul.

But on the other hand, when the bonds of sense are broken, and the believer enters the spiritual world, he comes nearer to spiritual objects, which are his chief good; his joy must thereby be increased. The consciousness of joy (and it may be, the more sensible impressions from the objects of his affections) will suggest the cause of the spiritual blessing that refreshes his mind. *That cause is Christ.* The laws of the mental nature unite Christ and glory in the sanctified spirit. Thus the circle of hallowed suggestion will be closed. Christ rules the soul by law, which makes him ever-present with his people; and, therefore, while law binds the unsanctified spirit to its sins, as to a body of death, it binds the believing mind to Christ forever. "The sting of death is sin; and the strength of sin is the law: but thanks be to God who giveth us the victory, through Jesus Christ our Lord." Amen and Amen.

Thus have we endeavored to exhibit "the evidence of the power, wisdom, and goodness of God; in the first place, from considerations independent of written Revelation; and, in the second place, from the Revelation of the Lord Jesus; and from the whole to point out the inferences most necessary and useful to mankind."

We think we have proved that the God of Nature is the God of Grace—that the Supreme good in God is the author of Christianity, and the supreme good in man its end.

ADDENDUM.

EXCURSES ON HYPOTHESES; ESPECIALLY THE HYPOTHESIS OF PRE-EXISTENCE.

An hypothesis which has no basis in phenomena, nor any in experience, is a mere speculation which may awaken interest by the ingenuity of its argument, or by the skill with which the writer selects and uses material in constructing his scheme. Such labor, however, can be of but little value in the realm of substantial thought. Some hypotheses, as mere figments of the fancy, may amuse—some, marked by the characteristics of an inquiring mind, may elicit thought upon an important subject, while some may be suggestive, and indicate to other minds trains of ideas which lead in the end to the acquisition of real knowledge.

The hypothesis of creation by law, which we have had occasion frequently to notice in the previous pages, attempts to save itself from reproach, by giving all the veracity which the author can procure, to the facts upon which his reasonings are predicated. This is wise, because if the foundation be not trustworthy, the superstructure can not be.

There are some hypotheses based wholly upon conjecture, and hence their authors do not have any trouble either with objective facts or subjective experience. A recent work, under the momentous title of the *Conflict of Ages!* by Dr. Edward Beecher, a gentleman of learning and piety, is a good example of that kind of hypothesis which is founded in the conjectures of an inquiring mind, and elaborated to fill the significance of its title.

If we could suppose Dr. Beecher to have fallen into the vein of Swift, we would be sure that the design of his book was to awaken the conviction that some of the older theologies were conceived in the shadow of a darker age, and can not be maintained in their *prima facie* interpretation, without offense to enlightened Christians of the present day. If this be the intention of the book, it will aid in accomplishing an end ; whether a beneficial one or not, it is not our business here to determine.

There should be some word in our language which would stand for those mere creations of the fancy, which are often called hypotheses, but which are predicated entirely upon conjectures. If we were to venture an addition to our already teeming vocabulary, we would suggest the composite word *pseudo-thesis*, as a proper one to designate this kind of writing. As in such cases it is not necessary (or rather, it is not expedient) to spend any time either with the facts of nature or of revelation, a tolerably active imagination might frame a *pseudo-thesis* which would appeal to the reason with as much plausibility as that of the excellent author of the "Conflict of Ages."

Let us look at the conflict from another stand-point —ascertain the difficulty to be solved, and try the force of our new definition.

We will assume a doctrine taught in the Bible, and one which is historically verified in the case of the Jews. *Children do suffer for the sins of their parents.* God is the creator and moral ruler of his creatures. Man is the creature of his power, and the subject of his providence. Then, if every man comes into the world a depraved moral being, and comes into the world at such times and in such circumstances as the Creator elects, how are the acts of the Creator in punishing children for the sins of their parents to be reconciled with the principles of "honor and right."

Here we postulate our *pseudo-thesis* in relation to the "Conflict of all Ages." We assume that men are created in races. Then each spirit that is created lives on upon the earth in successive bodies till the end of the race. When one body dies the spirit is transmitted into another, and so consecutively for ages. Thus the Jews, as their Rabbis, or Doctors of Divinity taught, were all created at the same time, and while they often change bodies, the spirits of the race continue upon the earth, the same in number and person. An opinion similar to this had not only the suffrage of very venerable and learned men among the ancients, but it is countenanced, likewise, by great names of modern times. Among these we might mention Herder, of Weimar.

Now we shall endeavor to maintain this view of the subject, and by it vindicate the Divine government from the charges of *dishonor* and *wrong*.

The Jews in the days of the Messiah committed their fearful sin. A curse came upon them and their descendants, and followed them seventeen hundred years. Now how shall we reconcile the "principles of honor and right," with the penal providences of God, and the facts of history, unless we suppose that the same spirits that committed the sin, suffered also the penalty? The reason reluctates—the conscience repels the idea that a Jew of the middle ages suffered for the sins of others who lived ten centuries before, and with whose acts the sufferer had no more connection than he had with the sin of Adam?

It may be answered that one generation approves of

all the acts of preceding generations of the same race, and therefore succeeding generations are guilty, in a good sense, for the crimes of those who preceded them. But this is not a true averment; because the Jews have not for many centuries believed that their fathers were actuated by the motives ascribed to them. But furthermore, allowing this to be true, the race-feeling is not of their own begetting. They did not choose to be born after the fact, nor to be born Jews. They had no agency in this matter, hence the principles of "honor and right" are still unsatisfied. If the reader of this page had been born a Jew, he would have had the same race-feeling which affects them. Who then shall reconcile with the "principles of honor and right," the fact that the Jews of the middle ages suffered for the acts of their race a thousand years before? It can be done, as we have already said, by assuming the continued life of the soul in a series of bodies during the whole existence of a race.

In behalf of this view of the subject, take the following facts and reasonings:

(*a*) The race-feeling continues the same; the mental and moral peculiarities, and prejudices, and proclivities, continue the same from generation to generation. This proves one of two things, either that the parents transmit their moral qualities to the child, or that a spirit possessing the same peculiarities lives in the new embodiment. Both of these may be true, because the moral peculiarities of the father are the same with others of his race.

(*b*) The physiognomy of the race in all ages has been the same. The seed produces the tree, and not the tree the seed, in all cases after the first: *so the soul moulds the body*. Each spirit assimilates matter, and produces the conformation and development of its own corporiety, in accordance with its own nature. Now, the phrenological, physiognomical, and physiological conformation of the Hebrews has been the same in all ages. This fact, in its scientific analysis, strikingly confirms the opinion that the same race of spirits develops the successive Jewish generations from age to age.

(*c*) Our scheme has likewise a more certain foundation in the Scriptures than any other view of "The Conflict of Ages." In Luke, chap. xi. 51, it is written: "From the blood of Abel unto the blood of Zacharias, which perished between the altar and the temple, verily I say unto you, it shall be required of this generation." Now, it is well known that the Jews recognize Abel as one of the progenitors of their race. And as "*Nott and Gliddon*" have intimated that Adam (or an Adam) was father of the Jews, we have therefore their authority on this point (and, as *courtesy* and *modesty* are always characteristics of profound and trustworthy thinkers, the authority of these philosophers should be weighed).

Now, as doctors of divinity among the Jews held the opinion that the spirits of the Jews were the same in all generations, is not this passage in Matthew, which speaks according to the *usus loquendi* of the times, a distinct authorization of our views ?

We may, then, affirm our *pseudo*-thesis to be a true *hypo*thesis, predicated, not only on a scientific, but a scriptural basis ; hence we infer that the retribution which fell upon the Jews, for many ages, was the desert of their moral transgressions, committed in *pre-existing bodies.*

(*d*) But the historico-moral argument for this scheme of vindicating "honor and right" in Divine Providence, has a force even more conclusive than some of the considerations before mentioned.

It is one of the doctrines of religion, which is abundantly supported by profane history, that nations do suffer in this world the consequences of their national sins. But those who suffer the penalty are generally separated many generations from those who perpetrated the evil for which the nation is punished. Now we submit the question to Dr. Beecher and the many respectable theologians of his school, how are the principles of honor and right to be vindicated if the penalty does not fall upon the criminals, but upon those who did not sin with them, nor fall with them, in the acts which corrupted the nation, and brought the penalty due to preceding generations upon the last one? The men have been dead a thousand years who perpetrated the first transgression, and it was their example and influence which encouraged the sins of their successors; unless, therefore, this last generation are personally guilty for the sins of the first generations, who induced the penalty, how can Dr. B. or any body else, vindicate Providence upon the principles of "honor and right?" But if the last generations were personally interested in the first transgressions—if they lived *in* their progenitors, and sinned *with* them in all their offenses, then they deserve to suffer personally the penalty for all the past. Thus, by our *pseudo*-thesis, the principles of honor and right in Providence are vindicated, and the "Conflict of Ages" adjusted, forever—or, if not *forever*, we think we have said enough to secure an armistice, at least, during the present century.

But whether the grand conflict be issued or not, arguments do not fail us in support of our proposition:

It is a principle of revelation, supported also by the spirit of human legislation in all ages, that sin should be repaid in kind: "Whatsoever measure ye meet shall be meeted unto you"—"He that taketh the sword shall fall by the sword." Now, providential judgments upon races are often strikingly in accordance with this principle. As an instance, take the case of the Spaniards, under Cortez and his *compirates.* They slew with the sword the ancient Mexicans, "conquered a peace," and appropriated their lands and wealth. The posterity of the conquerors established themselves in the country. Centuries pass; the conquerors still reign over their conquered possessions. But now God raises up another race against those ancient aggressors, and they suffer (*i. e.*, the *old* Spaniards in *new* bodies suffer) the same penalty which they had inflicted upon the Mexicans. They fall by the sword; and their territory is wrested from them *upon the same principles* which governed them when they wrested the same soil from the Aztecs.

Thus the principles of honor and right are vindicated by our *pseudo*-thesis in another form. We hope the author of the "Conflict" will himself accept this view, as it is not predicated in conjecture, but upon facts drawn from history, science, and Scripture.

We concede that one of the same objections may be

alleged against our view of the "Conflict" which meets the scheme of Dr. B. As man has no consciousness of having sinned in a preceding world, or in a preceding body, and as it is the effort of the *author* of the "Conflict" to reconcile the principles of honor and right, *as asserted by conscience and reason*, with the divine proceeding, it is difficult to see how the reconciliation is to be effected, while the penalty is inflicted where no consciousness of demerit exists.

But, in answer to this objection, our scheme has at least one hypothesis on its side. The author of the "Vestiges of the History of Creation" has, as he supposes, shown that the whole series of species which comprise the creation are one—that man is the complement of all; or, at least, that he is the head of the series. Now, as man has only in this age, by the aid of this author, reached the knowledge that he existed in past ages in the form of a shark, and thence upward to a baboon, and finally to a man, this conclusion, reached by this hypothesis, *is against* Dr. B.'s theory, but *not against* ours. If man came up from the *globator volvox*, through an evolving series of advancing species, then it is evident he did not sin *as man* in another state of existence. If men sinned at all in a former state of existence, it must have been as reptilia, or some other order of the lower carnivora.

Now, as the development theory has more facts of a certain sort to support it than the pre-existence theory, we hold it to be proved that our existence as sharks in a former state is more probable than our pre-existence as sinners, *f. e. d.*

In conclusion, may we be permitted to offer a serious suggestion to the writers of our day,* who are anxious to vindicate the Divine character from all complicity with the origin of evil. It is to be regretted that good men should lose time and labor on such questions ; but this they will do, while they admit into the discussion definitions and *dogmata* which are untrue both to science and revelation. If imperfection and evil are the same thing, having various relations, then all that is necessary to vindicate the Divine character is to reveal the Divine plan, and show the perfect end to which the creation is advancing. The origin of physical and moral evil (if we must assume such evils to exist) consists in those imperfections which exist in a process before it has reached maturity. To those whose minds can apprehend the perfect, there will appear evils in the present state of things. Man was made to perceive the future perfect, and to struggle for its attain-

* We do no more than justice to this class of writers when we say, that in it are often found good and able minds.

ment. *To him a sense of evil is good,* because it is necessary in the nature of things to stimulate to moral advancement, and in beings where there is no sense of evil, the evil exists only as imperfection belongs to a process which has not reached maturity.

VALUABLE WORKS

PUBLISHED BY

GOULD AND LINCOLN,

59 WASHINGTON STREET, BOSTON.

SACRED RHETORIC: Or, Composition and Delivery of Sermons. By HENRY J. RIPLEY, Prof. in Newton Theological Institution. Including Ware's Hints on Extemporaneous Preaching. Second thousand. 12mo, 75 cts.

An admirable work, clear and succint in its positions and recommendations, soundly based on good authority, and well supported by a variety of reading and illustrations. — *N. Y. Literary World.*

We have looked over this work with a lively interest. The arrangement is easy and natural, and the selection of thoughts under each topic very happy. The work is one that will command readers. It is a comprehensive manual of great practical utility. — *Phil. Ch. Chronicle.*

The author contemplates a man *preparing to compose a discourse* to promote the great ends of preaching, and unfolds to him the process through which his mind ought to pass. We commend the work to ministers, and to those preparing for the sacred office, as a book that will efficiently aid them in studying thoroughly the subject it brings before them. — *Phil. Ch. Observer.*

It presents a rich variety of rules for the practical use of the clergyman, and evinces the good sense, the large experience, and the excellent spirit of Dr. Ripley; and the whole volume is well fitted to instruct and stimulate the writer of sermons. — *Bibliotheca Sacra.*

An excellent work is here offered to theological students and clergymen. It is not a compilation, but is an original treatise, fresh, practical, and comprehensive, and adapted to the pulpit offices of the present day. It is full of valuable suggestions, and abounds with clear illustrations. — *Zion's Herald.*

It cannot be too frequently perused by those whose duty it is to *persuade* men. — *Congregationalist.*

Prof. Ripley possesses the highest qualifications for a work of this kind. His position has given him great experience in the peculiar wants of theological students. — *Providence Journal.*

His canons on selecting texts, stating the proposition, collecting and arranging materials, style, delivery, etc., are just and well stated. Every theological student to whom this volume is *accessible* will be likely to procure it. — *Christian Mirror, Portland.*

It is manifestly the fruit of mature thought and large observation; it is pervaded by a manly tone, and abounds in judicious counsels; it is compactly written and admirably arranged, both for study and reference. It will become a text book for theological students, we have no doubt: that it deserves to be read by all ministers is to us as clear. — *N. Y. Recorder.*

THE CHRISTIAN WORLD UNMASKED. By JOHN BERRIDGE, A. M., Vicar of Everton, Bedfordshire, Chaplain to the Right Hon. The Earl of Buchan, etc. *New Edition.* With Life of the Author, by the REV. THOMAS GUTHRIE, D. D., Minister of Free St. John's, Edinburgh. 16mo, cloth.

"The book," says DR. GUTHRIE, in his Introduction, "which we introduce anew to the public, has survived the test of years, and still stands towering above things of inferior growth like a cedar of Lebanon. Its subject is all important; in doctrine it is sound to the core; it glows with fervent piety; it exhibits a most skilful and unsparing dissection of the dead professor; while its style is so remarkable, that he who could *preach* as Berridge has *written*, would hold any congregation by the ears."

THE CHRISTIAN REVIEW. Edited by JAMES D. KNOWLES, BARNAS SEARS, and S. F. SMITH. 8 vols. Commencing with vol. one. Half cl., lettered, 8,00. Single volumes, (except the first,) may be had in numbers, 1,00.

These first eight volumes of the Christian Review contain valuable contributions from the leading men of the Baptist and several other denominations, and will be found a valuable acquisition to any library.

A4

PHILIP DODDRIDGE.

HIS LIFE AND LABORS.

A Centenary Memorial. By JOHN STOUHTON, D. D., author of "Spiritual Heroes," &c., and an INTRODUCTORY CHAPTER by REV. JAMES G. MIALL, author of "Footsteps of our Forefathers," &c. With beautiful Illuminated Title Page, Frontispiece, etc. 16mo, cloth, 60 cts.

Since the flood of biographies, memoirs, personal recollections, &c., with which the press teems at present, it is refreshing to get hold of a book like this.—*Presbyterian Witness.*

This is a clear, concise and interesting memoir of a man whose works and praise have been, for more than a century, in the churches on both sides of the Atlantic. The thousands who have read his "Rise and Progress of Religion," will want to know more of the author; and this volume is adapted to meet that want.—*Ch. Messenger.*

The sketch is drawn with remarkable literary skill, and the volume is one to be read with high satisfaction and profit. —*N. Y. Mirror.*

There are numerous readers who will rejoice in a volume that throws fresh light on the ministerial career and the writings of Dr. Doddridge. His great reputation as a religious author is chiefly based upon the celebrated work entitled, "The Rise and Progress of Religion in the soul," but he was no mean poet, and some of his hymns are unsurpassed.—*N. Y. Commercial.*

This works merits a place among the best Christian biographies of our times.—*Phil. Ch. Obs.*

We think nobody can read the book without feeling fresh admiration for Dr. Doddridge's character, and without being impressed with the conviction, that he was one of the finest models of the benevolent spirit of Christianity with which the world has been blessed since the days of the Apostle John.—*Puritan Recorder.*

THE LIFE AND CORRESPONDENCE OF JOHN FOSTER.

Author of "Decission of Character." Essays, etc. Edited by J. E. RYLAND, with notices of MR. FOSTER, as a Preacher and Companion. By JOHN SHEPPARD. A new edition, *two volumes in one*, 700 pages. 12mo, cloth, $1,25.

In simplicity of language, in majesty of conception, in the eloquence of that conciseness which conveys in a short sentence more meaning than the mind dares at once admit; his writings are unmatched.—*North British Review.*

It is with no ordinary expectations and gratification and delight that we have taken up the Biography and Correspondence of the author of the 'Essays on Decision of Character,' etc. The memoir of such a man as John Foster, must, of necessity, possess very peculiar attractions. A man whose writings have been perused with admiration wherever the English language is spoken or understood; whose calm, transparent and impressive thoughts have, in their acquaintance and contact, cut out new channels of thought in ten thousand other minds; whose dignified and sober views of life, religion, and immortality are adapted to shed so hallowed a spirit over all who become familiar with them. Mr. Ryland, the editor of the memorials, is favorably known on both sides of the water by his literary offerings; and in compilation of these volumes he has exercised a discriminating judgment, a blameless taste, and sound discretion.

We are glad to find ourselves in possession of so much additional matter from the well-nigh inspired pen of this great master in English composition.—*Christian Review.*

A book rich in every way—in good sense, vivacity, suggestiveness, liberality, and piety.—*Mirror.*

The letters which principally compose this volume, bears strongly the impress of his own original mind, and is often characterized by a depth and power of thought rarely met with even in professedly elaborate disquisitions.—*Albany Argus.*

Mr. Foster was one of the most admirable writers of England. His life is full of instruction, and will prove of great value to those young ministers whose labors are attended with poor success. The fame and influence of Foster will live as long as talent, learning, and piety shall be respected on the earth. We commend, therefore, most heartily, the work before us to the public. We commend it to the scholar, and assure him that in the correspondence of Mr. Foster, he will find letters of rare literary worth, and much to improve his taste and his mind. We sincerely hope that all our clergymen will procure this book, and read it—read it often. We know of no work which will do more for their literary culture.—*N. Y. Ch. Messenger.*

John Foster was one of the strongest writers of his age.—*Christian Register.*

This work must constitute the choice book of the season, in the department of correspondence and biography. We all wish to know what he was as a friend, a husband, a father, and as a practical exponent of what is enshrined in the immortal productions of his pen. All will rejoice in the opportunity of adding this treasure to their libraries.—*Watchman and Reflector.*

MIALL'S WORKS.

FOOTSTEPS OF OUR FOREFATHERS; what they Suffered and what they Sought. Describing Localities and portraying Personages and Events conspicuous in the Struggles for Religious Liberty. By JAMES G. MIALL, author of "Memorials of Early Christianity," etc. Containing thirty-six fine Illustrations. 12mo, 1,00.

An exceedingly entertaining work. It is full of strong points. The reader soon catches the fire and zeal of those sterling men whom we have so long admired, and ere he is aware becomes so deeply enlisted in their cause that he finds it difficult to lay aside the book till finished. — *Ch. Parlor Mag.*

A book to stir one's spirit to activity and self-sacrifice in the work of God. It portrays the character, the deeds, the sufferings, and the success of those heroic non-conformists who stood up for the truth against tyranny. It is a book worthy of a large sale. — *Zion's Herald.*

A work absorbingly interesting, and very instructive. — *Western Lit. Magazine.*

The title of this book attracted our attention; its contents have held us fast to its pages to the very close. Its story is of principles and sufferings with which every American who prizes his birthright, and would know how it has been secured, should be familiar. It embraces graphic sketches of localities and scenes, of personages and events, illustrative of the grand struggle for religious liberty. It is fascinating in style, and reliable for substance. It is full of antiquarian lore, and abounds in charming local descriptions. Most earnestly do we recommend it. — *Watchman and Reflector.*

The events narrated and scenes described by the author give us interesting and impressive views of the great sacrifices made by the noble sufferers for the priceless boon of spiritual freedom, which American citizens claim as their birthright. — *Ch. Observer.*

This volume is devoted to biographical notices of those noble minds who made the grand discoveries of civil and religious liberty in England, and who counted not their lives dear, so that the Bible and the freedom of conscience should descend upon their children's children. The anecdotes of these men and their times are full of interest, and are drawn from the most authentic sources. — *Nat. Intel.*

This is a most captivating book, and one that the reader is compelled to finish if he once begins it. We really wish that every family in our land could have a copy. It has kept us perfectly enchained from beginning to end. — *Newport Observer.*

MEMORIALS OF EARLY CHRISTIANITY; Presenting, in a graphic, compact, and popular Form, Memorable Events of Early Ecclesiastical History, etc. By JAMES G MIALL, author of "Footsteps of our Forefathers," etc. With numerous elegant Illustrations. 12mo, cloth, 1,00.

☞ This, like the "Footsteps of our Forefathers," will be found a work of uncommon interest.

We thank Mr. Miall for this volume, which our publishers have reprinted in quite handsome style. There are plain truths plainly told in this volume about ancient Christianity and the practices of the Christians of ante-Nicene times which we could wish *churchmen* would lay to heart and profit by. — *Episcopal Register.*

It is well written, *more* interesting than a *romance*, and yet full of instruction and warning for the present generation. — *Hartford Times.*

A work of no ordinary value as a faithful exponent of early church history, and we can most cheerfully commend it to all. Every Sabbath school should be supplied with copies of it. — *Ch. Secretary.*

Mr. Miall is a Congregational minister in England, and a popular writer of unusual power. He has the power of graphic delineation, and has given us pictures of early Christianity which have the charm of life and reality. We regard the volume as one of unusual interest and value, and our readers are assured that its glowing pages will excite their admiration. — *N. Y. Recorder.*

This is an extremely interesting work, embodying classic and ecclesiastic lore, and calculated to do much good by bringing the church of *to-day* into closer acquaintanceship and sympathy with the church of the early past. — *Congregationalist.*

A very successful attempt to *popularize* the history of the church during the first three centuries. The *results* of extended research are offered to the general reader in a style of *uncommon interest.* The mass of readers know far too little on church history. — *Watchman and Reflector.*

We have in this volume, embodied in a lucid and attractive form, some of the most important facts of early ecclesiastical history, in illustration of the original purity and power of Christian faith. It is a work of labor, and labor very successfully applied. — *Puritan Recorder.*

A volume of thrilling interest. It takes the reader through a very important period of secular and ecclesiastical history. We are glad to see this work. It cannot fail of doing good. — *Western Lit. Messenger.*

THE PREACHER AND THE KING;

OR, BOURDALOUE IN THE COURT OF LOUIS XIV.

Being an Account of that distinguished Era. Translated from the French of L. BUNGENER. Paris, fourteenth edition. With an Introduction, by the REV. GEORGE POTTS, D. D., New York. 12mo, cloth, 1,25.

It combines *substantial history with the highest charm of romance;* the most rigid philosophical criticism with a thorough analysis of human character and faithful representation of the spirit and manners of the age to which it relates. We regard the book as a valuable contribution to the cause not merely of general literature, but especially of pulpit eloquence. Its attractions are so various that it can hardly fail to find readers of almost every description. — *Puritan Recorder.*

A very delightful book. It is full of interest, and equally replete with sound thought and profitable sentiment. — *N. Y. Commercial.*

It is a volume at once curious, instructive, and fascinating. The interviews of Bourdaloue and Claude, and those of Bossuet, Fenelon, and others, are remarkably attractive, and of finished taste. Other high personages of France are brought in to figure in the narrative, while rhetorical rules are exemplified in a manner altogether new. Its extensive sale in France is evidence enough of its extraordinary merit and its peculiarly attractive qualities. — *Ch. Advocate.*

It is full of life and animation, and conveys a graphic idea of the state of morals and religion in the Augustan age of French literature. — *N. Y. Recorder.*

This book will attract by its novelty, and prove particularly engaging to those interested in the pulpit eloquence of an age characterized by the flagrant wickedness of Louis XIV. The author has exhibited singular skill in weaving into his narrative sketches of the remarkable men who flourished at that period, with original and striking remarks on the subject of preaching. — *Presbyterian.*

Its historical and biographical portions are valuable; its comments excellent, and its effect pure and benignant. A work which we recommend to all, as possessing rare interest. — *Buffalo Morn. Exp.*

A book of rare interest, not only for the singular ability with which it is written, but for the graphic account which it gives of the state of pulpit eloquence during the celebrated era of which it treats. It is perhaps the best biography extant of the distinguished and eloquent preacher, who above all others most pleased the king; while it also furnishes many interesting particulars in the lives of his professional contemporaries. We content ourself with warmly commending it. — *Savannah Journal.*

The author is a minister of the Reformed Church. In the forms of narrative and conversations, he portrays the features and character of that remarkable age, and illustrates the claims and duties of the sacred office, and the important ends to be secured by the eloquence of the pulpit. — *Phil. Ch. Obs.*

A book which unfolds to us the private conversation, the interior life and habits of study of such men as Claude, Bossuet, Bourdaloue, Massillon, and Bridaine, cannot but be a precious gift to the American church and ministers. It is a book full of historical facts of great value, sparkling with gems of thought, polished scholarship, and genuine piety. — *Cin. Ch. Advocate.*

This volume presents a phase of French life with which we have never met in any other work. The author is a minister of the Reformed Church in Paris, where his work has been received with unexampled popularity, having already gone through *fourteen* editions. The writer has studied not only the divinity and general literature of the age of Louis XIV., but also the memories of that period, until he is able to reproduce a life-like picture of society at the Court of the Grand Monarch. — *Alb. Trans.*

A work which we recommend to all, as possessing rare interest. — *Buffalo Ev. Express.*

In form it is descriptive and dramatic, presenting the reader with animated conversations between some of the most famous preachers and philosophers of the Augustan age of France. The work will be read with interest by all intelligent men; but it will be of especial service to the ministry, who cannot afford to be ignorant of the facts and suggestions of this instructive volume. — *N. Y. Ch. Intel.*

The work is very fascinating, and the lesson under its spangled robe is of the gravest moment to every pulpit and every age. — *Ch. Intelligencer.*

THE PRIEST AND THE HUGUENOT; or Persecution in the Age of Louis XV. Part I., A Sermon at Court; Part II., A Sermon in the City; Part III., A Sermon in the Desert. Translated from the French of L. BUNGENER, author of "The Preacher and the King." 2 vols. 12mo, cloth. ☞ *A new Work.*

☞ This is truly a masterly production, full of interest, and may be set down as one of the greatest Protestant works of the age.

WORKS BY DR. TWEEDIE.

GLAD TIDINGS; or, The Gospel of Peace. A series of Daily Meditations for Christian Disciples. By Rev. W. K. TWEEDIE, D. D. With an elegant Illustrated Title-page. 16mo, cloth. 63 cents.

These meditations, though brief, are comprehensive and weighty. It is remarkable for condensation, for a deep evangelical tone, and for putting itself into direct contact with the conscience and the heart. — *Albany Argus.*

We heartily wish this little book were in every Christian family, and could be carefully read through by every Christian. — *N. Y. Evangelist.*

This sweet little volume challenges our warmest commendation. Every page glows with Christian example and goodness. The perusal of one chapter will awake a keener relish for the commencement of another. The *Frontispiece*, representing the shepherd's watch of their flocks by night, is sublimely beautiful. — *Lawrence Courier.*

Earnest and pointed in style, pithy and practical in thought, thoroughly evangelical, it is not only a useful but a valuable work. — *Religious Herald.*

A LAMP TO THE PATH; or, the Bible in the Heart, the Home, and the Market-place. With an elegant Illustrated Title-page. 16mo, cloth. 63 cents.

The power, the beauty, and the necessity of religion in the heart, the home, the workshop, the market-place, the professions, and in social intercourse, are happily illustrated, and no person can read the work without being greatly benefited. It is a jewel, and should enrich every family library. The last chapter, entitled, "Religion the Crown and Glory of Man's Life," is worthy of being engraven, as with the point of a diamond, on every human heart. — *Southern Literary Messenger.*

We wish every family could read the volume. Society, in that event, would owe a debt of gratitude to the author for many a personal reformation. — *Peterson's Magazine.*

This little volume brings Christianity home to the bosoms and business of men. It is a lucid, impressive, and beautiful exposition of Christian obligations. — *Albany Argus.*

It is eloquently written, with a searching closeness as well as rare correctness of style; and both young men and old may ponder over its pages with profit. — *Yankee Blade.*

SEED-TIME AND HARVEST; or, Sow Well and Reap Well. A Book for the Young. With an elegant Illustrated Title-page. 16mo, cloth. 63 cents.

An excellent little book, more particularly designed for the information and religious improvement of young readers; but persons of all ages may derive pleasure and profit from its perusal. — *New York Commercial.*

The great thought which this work is designed to, and does very successfully, develop, comes out on the title-page. No person can read it attentively, without feeling that there is an importance attached even to what seem to be his most indifferent actions. — *Puritan Recorder.*

A most precious volume this to the young, taking their first step and first look in life; teaching them, in language at once simple and elevated, that if they would reap well, they must sow well; that if they would enjoy an old age of honor, they must be trained in youth to virtue. — *Dr. Sprague, Albany Spectator.*

The object of this little book is to impress the young with the great truth "that whatsoever a man soweth, that shall he also reap;" showing also "how much depends upon a single principle adopted or a single deed done" in early life. We hope it will have many readers. — *Ch. Herald.*

THE MORN OF LIFE; or, Examples of Female Excellence. A Book for Young Ladies. 16mo, cloth. *In press.*

☞ The above works, by Dr. Tweedie, are of uniform size and style. They are most charming, pious, and instructive works, beautifully gotten up, and well adapted for "gift-books."

FAMILY WORSHIP; or, the Morning and Evening Sacrifice. One volume. Octavo, cloth. *In press.* (h)

WORKS JUST ISSUED.

VISITS TO EUROPEAN CELEBRITIES. By WILLIAM B. SPRAGUE, D. D. 12mo. Cloth. $1.00. Second Edition.

THE first edition of this work was exhausted within a short time after its publication. It consists of a series of Personal Sketches, *drawn from life*, of many of the most distinguished men and women of Europe, with whom the author became acquainted in the course of several European tours: Edward Irving, Rowland Hill, Wilberforce, Jay, Robert Hall, John Foster, Hannah More, Guizot, Louis Philippe, Sismondi, Tholuck, Gesenius, Neander, Humboldt, Encke, Rogers, Campbell, Joanna Baillie, John Pye Smith, Amelia Opie, Dr. Pusey, Mrs. Sherwood, Maria Edgeworth, John Galt, Dr. Wardlaw, Dr. Chalmers, Sir David Brewster, Lord Jeffrey, Professor Wilson, (Kit North,) Southey, and others, are here portrayed as the author saw them in their own homes, and under the most advantageous circumstances. Accompanying the Sketches are the AUTOGRAPHS of each of the personages described. This unique feature of the work adds in no small degree to its attractions. For the social circle, for the traveller by railroad and steamboat, for all who desire to be refreshed and not weared by reading, the book will prove to be a most agreeable companion. The public press of all shades of opinion, North and South, have given it a most flattering reception.

THE STORY OF THE CAMPAIGN. A Complete Narrative of the War in Southern Russia. Written in a Tent in the Crimea. By Major E. BRUCE HAMLEY, Author of "Lady Lee's Widowhood." 12mo. Thick. Printed Paper Covers. 37½ Cents.

Contents.—The Rendezvous—The Movement to the Crimea—First Operations in the Crimea—Battle of the Alma—The Battle-field—The Katcha and the Balbek—The Flank March—Occupation of Balaklava—The Position before Sebastopol—Commencement of the Siege—Attack on Balaklava—First Action of Inkermann—Battle of Inkermann—Winter on the Plains—Circumspective—The Hospitals on the Bosphorus—Exculpatory—Progress of the Siege—The Burial Truce—View of the Works.

THIS was first published in *Blackwood's Magazine*, in which form it has attracted general attention. It is the only connected and continuous narrative of the War in Europe that has yet appeared. The author is an officer of rank in the British army, and has borne an active part in the campaign; he has also won a brilliant reputation as the author of the fascinating story of "Lady Lee's Widowhood." By his profession of arms, by his actual participation in the conflict, and by his literary abilities, he is qualified in a rare degree, for the task he has undertaken. The expectations thus raised will not be disappointed. To those who have been dependent on the brief, fragmentary, interrupted, and irresponsible newspaper notices of the war, this book will furnish a full, complete, graphic, and perfectly reliable account from the beginning. Should the author's life be spared, his history of future operations will follow, and will be issued by the publishers uniform with the present volume.

ROGET'S THESAURUS OF ENGLISH WORDS. A New and Improved Edition. 12mo. Cloth. $1.50.

THIS edition is based on the last London edition (just issued.) The first American edition having been prepared by Dr. Sears, for strictly educational pur poses, those words and phrases, properly termed "vulgar," incorporated into the original work, were omitted. Regret having been expressed by critics and scholars, whose opinions are entitled to respect, at this omission, in the present new edition the expurgated portions have been restored, but by such an arrangement of matter as not to interfere with the educational purpose of the American editor. Besides this, there will be important additions of words and phrases not in the Eng lish edition, making this, therefore, in all respects, more full and perfect than the author's edition.

NEW WORKS

THE TEACHER'S LAST LESSON. A MEMOIR OF MARTHA WHITING, late of the Charlestown Female Seminary, consisting chiefly of Extracts from her Journal, interspersed with Reminisences and Suggestive Reflections. By CATHARINE N. BADGER, an Associate Teacher. With a Portrait, and an Engraving of the Seminary. 12mo. Cloth. $1.00. Second Edition.

THE subject of this Memoir was, for a quarter of a century, at the head of one of the most celebrated Female Seminaries in the country. During that period she educated more than *three thousand* young ladies. She was a kindred spirit to Mary Lyon, the celebrated founder of Mount Holyoke Seminary, with whom, for strength of character, eminent piety, devotion to her calling, and extraordinary success therein, she well deserves to be ranked.

MY MOTHER: or Recollections of Maternal Influence. By a NEW ENGLAND CLERGYMAN. 12mo. Cloth. 75 Cents.

THIS is a new and enlarged edition of a work that was first published in 1849. It passed rapidly through three editions, when the sale was arrested by the embarrassment of the publisher. The author has now revised it, and added another chapter, so that it comes before the public with the essential claims of a new work. . . . It is the picture of a quiet New England family, so drawn and colored as to subserve the ends of *domestic education*. The central figure is the author's mother, around whom are grouped the various members of the family. Biographical sketches and lessons of practical wisdom are so intermingled, that while the former relieve the latter, these in turn give force and significance to the sketches. . . . . . . The author has already distinguished himself in various walks of literature, but from motives of delicacy towards the still surviving characters of the book, he chooses for the present to conceal his name. . . . . . A writer of wide celebrity says of the book, in a note to the publisher — " It is one of those rare pictures, painted from life, with the exquisite skill of one of the *old masters*, which so seldom present themselves to the amateur."

WORKS IN PREPARATION.

MEMOIR OF OLD HUMPHREY. With Gleanings from his Portfolio, and a Portrait.

KNOWLEDGE IS POWER. A View of the Productive Forces of Modern Society, and the Results of Labor, Capital and Skill. By CHARLES KNIGHT. With numerous Illustrations. American Edition. Revised, with additions, by DAVID A. WELLS, Editor of the " Annual of Scientific Discovery."

SACRED LATIN POETRY. CHIEFLY LYRICAL. Selected and arranged for use. With Notes and an Introduction by RICHARD CHENEVIX TRENCH. Revised, with important Additions by J. L. LINCOLN, Professor of the Latin Language in Brown University.

EXPOSITION OF THE SERMON ON THE MOUNT. Drawn from the Writings of St. Augustine, with Observations. By RICHARD CHENEVIX TRENCH.

☞ G. & L. would call attention to their extensive list of publications, embracing valuable works in THEOLOGY, SCIENCE, LITERATURE AND ART; TEXT BOOKS FOR SCHOOLS AND COLLEGES, and MISCELLANEOUS, etc., in large variety, the productions of some of the ablest writers and most scientific men of the age, among which will be found those of Chambers, Hugh Miller, Agassiz, Gould, Guyot, Marcou, Dr. Harris, Dr. Wayland, Dr. Williams, Dr. Ripley, Dr. Kitto, Dr. Tweedie, Dr. Choules, Dr. Sprague, Newcomb, Banvard, " Walter Aimwell," Bungener, Miall, Archdeacon Hare, and others of like standing and popularity, and to this list they are constantly adding. (o)

www.ingramcontent.com/pod-product-compliance
Lightning Source LLC
LaVergne TN
LVHW010216110826
845151LV00004B/1098

* 9 7 8 1 4 2 5 5 2 7 4 4 0 *